The Book of
Garden Ornament

Dedication

To my wife, Cynthia, without whose help I would not have been able to select the photographs in this book from the many thousands which were sent to me.

The Book of Garden Ornament

edited by Peter Hunt

J. M. Dent and Sons Limited London

First published 1974

© Text, J. M. Dent & Sons Ltd, 1974

Made in Great Britain
at the
Aldine Press · Letchworth · Herts
for
J. M. Dent & Sons Ltd
Aldine House · Albemarle Street · London

ISBN : 0 460 07695 7

Contents and List of Illustrations

Part II Garden Buildings

Editor's Preface

Nearly fifty years have elapsed since I was taken, as a small boy, to visit someone else's garden. It is so long ago that I cannot even remember which garden it was, though I can recall the broad stretches of lawn, great trees, statues, flower-filled urns, garden buildings and various other features.

Since then, particularly in the last twenty-five years, I have visited hundreds of gardens in Britain, various European countries and the United States of America, usually carrying a camera and a notebook to record my impressions.

At first the plants concerned me most; later I became interested in the general subject of garden design, read much of what had been written about it in the past two or three hundred years and, when the opportunity arose, compared what had been written with the actual garden. Eventually I became absorbed in what John Worlidge in *The Art of Gardening in Three Books* (1677) called 'invegetate Ornaments', all those fixed features which separately or together help to make great gardens what they are. And, by 'great' I do not necessarily mean large, for even small gardens can be great or notable and depend, to some extent, upon the correct placing of an 'invegetate Ornament'. By the standards of Stourhead, Chatsworth, Castle Howard or Studley Royal, Tintinhull in Somerset is a small garden, indeed, yet much of its beauty and interest derive from the careful placing of a few well-chosen ornaments, and just as Stourhead and Studley Royal and many other gardens appeal to hundreds of thousands of people, many of whom, like me, return to them time and again, because the ornaments, mainly garden buildings, are perfectly placed in the landscape, so does one return to Tintinhull and other equally small, intimate gardens.

This interest in 'invegetate Ornament' has led to this book; an attempt to describe and illustrate the various types of ornament that can be used to decorate gardens both large and small. To some extent the book is backward looking in that many of the features described and illustrated are 'classical' in concept. However, modern ornaments are well represented and I hope that garden designers, whether professional or amateur, will find some inspiration in the photographs and the accompanying text.

Gardening knows no frontiers and the ornaments represented come from many different countries, though I regret the absence of pictures showing features in the great gardens of Russia and other Eastern European countries, many of which have been restored to something approaching their former glory and are used as 'People's Parks'.

Many of the British gardens mentioned or illustrated in this book are open to the public, either regularly or occasionally. Some are National Trust properties and details of these and their opening arrangements may be obtained by writing to the Trust at 42 Queen Anne's Gate, London SW1H 9AS (details of Scottish properties are obtainable from the National Trust for Scotland, 5 Charlotte Square, Edinburgh EH2 4DU). A few properties are in the care of the Department of the Environment, the address of which is Neville House, Page Street, London SW1. However, the vast majority of gardens are privately owned and are opened mainly for charities. One of the main ones is the National Gardens Scheme (organized by the Queen's Institute of District Nursing), which publishes annually *Gardens of England and Wales Open to the Public*, giving opening times for over 1,200 gardens. This is obtainable from the Organizing Secretary, The National Gardens Scheme, 57 Lower Belgrave Street, London SW1W 0LR. In addition many gardens are open for gardeners' charities; details of these may be found in *Gardens to Visit*, published by the Gardeners Sunday Organization and is obtainable from the Organizer, White Witches, Claygate Road, Dorking, Surrey.

Some gardens are opened to the public to provide funds for their maintenance. Details of these, and many other gardens open from time to time, will be found in *Historic Houses, Castles and Gardens in Great Britain and Ireland*, published annually by ABC Travel Guides Ltd, and, like the two booklets mentioned above, obtainable also from bookstalls.

Finally, those who are interested in any aspect of the history of gardens and gardening should join the Garden History Society. The Society advises on the restoration of historic gardens, publishes a Journal, *Garden History*, three times a year and, among other activities, organizes visits to gardens of historic interest in Britain and abroad, many of which are seldom, if ever, open to the public. Inquiries should be addressed to the Secretary, Mrs Mavis Batey, 12 Charlbury Road, Oxford.

Elham,
1973.

PETER HUNT.

Foreword

by G. A. Jellicoe, CBE, FRIBA, MIPI, PPILA

There is no one who does not enjoy the first walk through a garden that he has not previously seen. There is perhaps first the pleasure of the disposition of space, whether open or enclosed, architectural or green. Then follows the appreciation of detail, of planting of all kinds and of formal ornament. It is mainly with the last that this book is concerned, and its interest will depend almost entirely on the reader's own inclination and understanding. The reader is divided, if one may so describe him, into three main categories. There are those who get nothing but pleasure through the enjoyment of the senses of sight, touch, smell and sometimes sound; and these (until recently at least) have been in the majority. Secondly, there are those with the possessive instinct, who would like to possess similar objects in their own gardens. Thirdly (and perhaps it is this category with which the contributors are most concerned), there are the discerning and creative who are able to put what they see through their own aesthetic digestion, and re-create.

For the first and perhaps most lovable category, the exploration of this book will be some compensation for not visiting the real thing. The size of the category can be appreciated from the huge number of visitors to gardens that are open to the public.

Until recently the second category, of those who wished to possess or to copy, far exceeded those who wished to create. In England particularly it was almost a universal sign of good taste to make gardens that were an echo of history. Except in the hands of an able and inventive practitioner such as Sir Edwin Lutyens, nearly all gardens were backward looking and sentimental, a taste pandered to by the commercial firms who produced, in addition to gnomes, reproductions of garden ornament by the mass. During this period, which corresponded roughly to the first half of this century, the other countries in Europe, notably in Scandinavia, were evolving a new garden culture more expressive of the age and, therefore, ultimately more satisfying.

In the third category is the reader (or visitor) who is only interested in a living art, but who is wise enough to turn to history for a deep rather than superficial appreciation. He will, for instance, know that a rich Renaissance vase is an extension of the human figure in its contemporary costume, and that its purpose as ornament at that time was quite different from its purpo se today: today it might express the personality or ethos of its environment, which is something quite different and harder to define. He will be percepti ve enough to be able to separate *form* from *content,* and to know that, however much he may enrich himself with detail, this in itself does not constitute garden design. If he is interested in the contemporary arts of painting and sculpture, he will not turn away with disgust from abstract art, but realize that the inquiring artist has temporarily abandoned 'content' in his search for pure 'form'. Pure form is primarily an appeal to the subconscious. The danger with garden art is that content, as illustrated especially in this book (and all the more because it is familiar), is so powerful a visual factor that the greater element of design, that of form, might be forgotten; a sense of form permeated classical gardens of all ages.

Keeping all this in mind, the discerning reader may explore the historic and modern examples shown in this book, happy in the assurance that they have been selected with care and discrimination, and in the knowledge that a true and not a superficial appreciation of the past sets a standard of immeasurable value for the future.

Acknowledgments

Apart from thanking those who have supplied photographs for this book, the editor and publishers wish to thank the following for their help in providing information:

Alton Towers Ltd; The Lord Astor of Hever; Major E. Bainbridge Copnall; Mrs Mavis Batey; Geoffrey Beard Esq.; Lady Irene Burton; Miss J. Butler; The Cement and Concrete Association; The late H. F. Clark; George Clarke Esq.; Major E. R. S. Compton; Compton Acres Ltd; Miss Cornelia Cremers; Anthony Dent Esq.; The Department of Conservation and Development, North Carolina; The Deputy Director of Agriculture, Lahore; The Director, Colonial Williamsburg, Virginia; The Director, Dumbarton Oaks, Washington, D.C.; The Director, Longwood Gardens, Pennsylvania; The Director, Tennessee Botanical Gardens; H. F. Dodson Esq., Hodnet Hall; The Marchioness of Dufferin and Ava; The late Mrs Margery Fish; The French Government Tourist Office; The Garden History Society; The Gartendirektor, Schloss Nymphenburg; Gimpel Fils Ltd; Miles Hadfield Esq., Hanover Gallery, London; Harlow Development Corporation; The late Sir John Heathcoat Amory, Bt.; The late Lord Heytesbury; George Howard Esq.; Anthony Huxley Esq.; T. B. Huxley Jones Esq.; IBM Corporation, Armonk, New York; Major Sir Joslyn Ingilby, Bt.; The Instutt for Hagenkunst, N.L.H., Vollebekk, Norway; The Keeper, Scottish National Gallery of Modern Art, Edinburgh; Mr & Mrs K. Jaggers; Major Arthur James; Mrs Susan Jellicoe; Colonel F. Lane Fox; The Librarian, Kent County Library, Maidstone; Raymond Lister Esq.; The London Library; F. W. H. Loudon Esq.; Mallett at Bourdon House Ltd; Marlborough Fine Arts Ltd, London; The Marlborough Gallery, New York; Leonard Manasseh Esq.; Professor Hermann Mattern; K. P. Mayer Esq.; Mono Concrete Ltd; The National Trust for Places of Historic Interest or Natural Beauty; The National Trust for Scotland; The Lord Northbourne; R. J. Pearn Esq.; Charles Puddle Esq.; Alan Roger Esq.; The Royal Society of British Sculptors; John Skelton Esq.; Stead H. Stead-Ellis Esq.; Graham Stuart Thomas Esq.; Sir Richard Sykes, Bt.; The Reverend Henry Thorold; The Virginia Chamber of Commerce; E. D. Wainwright Esq.; The late J. D. U. Ward; Sir Clough Williams-Ellis.

PART I
Ornaments and Decorations

Introduction

The human race has a desire—as powerful in the aboriginal as it is in the twentieth-century suburban Joneses—not to leave well alone but to add decoration; and the meaning of the verb 'to decorate', be it noted, is 'to adorn or beautify'. An attempt to define *those* two words brings us at once to the question of taste, and fashion in taste. The Neo-Georgians despised that of the Victorians, and now the New Elizabethans are bowing before the Victorians. One must, therefore, be neutral in discussing the subject.

Presumably garden decoration has evolved from the erection of religious symbols, and memorials to various gods or mythical (and subsequently human) heroes. Gardens throughout the world now contain such objects, sometimes in their original situations but more frequently torn out of their first context and transported far from their homes.

In the West we can certainly go back to the ornamentation of gardens in Roman times. The unburied gardens of Pompeii alone show many examples, of which a large proportion have yet earlier classical allusions. A religious symbol that has undergone a strange transformation is the so-called pineapple, particularly in favour during the eighteenth and early nineteenth centuries in the British Isles and also the United States. It is found in much earlier gardens such as Aranjuez in Spain and in many Italian gardens of the seventeenth century. It is now usually associated with the tropical fruit, but is in reality the cone of the stone-pine (*Pinus pinea*) of the Mediterranean lands which, on account of its large and numerous seeds, stood as a symbol of fertility in the Roman cult of Mithras. In the British Isles this faith was held particularly among the Roman legionaries who garrisoned the northern regions, and it is from among Roman remains in this cold part of the world that 'pineapple' finials have been dug up which are quite similar to, and the lineal ancestors of, the shining white pineapples that contrasted so pleasantly with the warm red brick of many a prosperous Georgian merchant's mansion.

The familiar pine-cone ornament is one whose significance can be easily traced. The original implication of others may be lost to us, but it is well to recall with the poet Marvell that

. . . statues polished by some ancient hand,
May to adorn the gardens stand;
But howso'er the figures do excel,
The Gods themselves do with us dwell.

In classical times the idea embodied in these lines had a literal meaning, and for the contemporary educated man the erection of all such statues and symbols was the serious expression of a whole body of myth and lore.

In the Orient also garden ornament has more than decorative importance. Josiah Conder tells us in *Landscape Gardening in Japan* that the celebrated stone lanterns which are a feature of Japanese garden design originated (so the legend went) in the beginning of the seventh century, when the Emperor's son, Prince Iruhiko, placed one in a solitary lake-side spot to protect wayfarers against robbers. Presumably because this stratagem was successful, it later became the custom for princes and nobles to present these lanterns as votive offerings to Buddhist temples and mausolea.

Although Japanese garden art is descended, and evolves, from the Chinese, the lantern is not known in China. Presumably, however, we may grant the Chinese their dragons. These creatures, their anatomical structure, symbolism and other qualities have been considerably studied by sinologists, and it can be confidently assumed that the owners of Chinese dragons who today use them as garden ornaments are rarely aware of their original quality, material or spiritual, which was quite unlike, and much more genial than, the significance attached to them in Western minds, for originally they were creatures regarded with affection rather than fear.

There can be no doubt that the architectural ornamentation of European gardens develops from Rome through the splendour of the Italian Renaissance gardens, and then in turn through Italy to France, culminating in the formal gardens of the period of Le Nôtre. Eliminating fountains, which are discussed at length in Section 2, life is given to the complex decoration by statuary. Gods, goddesses, caesars, satyrs, boys, dolphins, lions all abound, and form the major ornaments with, as it were, a personality of their own.

The formal or architectural garden obviously has numerous fundamental elements in its structure which particularly lend themselves to decoration. The inevitable containment within a closed area involves walls, and means of passing through them. The walls themselves are frequently decorated; they may be surmounted by elaborate coping, or their surface may be broken by niches and alcoves. Gateways are often most magnificent structures, the gates themselves, of elaborate open metalwork, giving a sense both of security to those within and of prohibition to those without, while their transparency encourages inquisitiveness and offers an invitation.

The variety of levels means stairways, raised passage-ways and protective balustrading. The newel-posts on stairs are often richly ornamental, while the form of the balusters and the moulding of their bases and rails can be superb pieces of design, as may the finials.

Isolated or grouped columns can be used for dramatic effect, or ranged in rows to form pergolas—appropriate enough in a hot sunny climate, but more effective as a setting for climbing plants in the north.

In the great Italian gardens all these works were designed by the leading artists of the day in the contemporary fashion and made by master-craftsmen; the names and works of many of these men are known.

In addition to the ornamentation of these integral parts of the structure, there was much else of a more portable nature. Such were the large stone or terra-cotta troughs, often elaborately carved, the *giardinerie* in which clipped trees were grown. Vases containing plants were perched regularly along the tops of walls and balustrades. Benches and seats were another more utilitarian form of decoration.

Certain Italian gardens were decorated by the display of statuary and comparable works of art from the valued collections of their owners. That of Cardinal Andrea della Valle in his Roman garden was already famous in 1540; the eighteenth-century collection of Cardinal Albani had the doubtful honour of being pillaged by Napoleon. The tradition has continued to this day in many parts of the world. A singularly fine example is that made by the late Harold Peto at Iford Manor in Wiltshire.

Nor should we forget the Italian mastery of the fantastic—indeed, horrific. This was displayed in the sixteenth-century garden at Bomarzo with its elephants, giant tortoises, bears, and representation of the mouth of hell itself.

The general principles underlying the design of these Italian gardens and their ornamentation were laid down by Alberti in his *Ten Books of Architecture*, published in 1485, and from then on they were developed with ever-increasing elaboration and freedom.

In due course the Renaissance manner spread northwards and was modified, indeed transformed, by the French to produce the most highly organized and finely detailed formal garden design ever known—a style that spread far beyond France, and one not eclipsed until the English natural manner became international in the late eighteenth century.

We have, therefore, the interesting situation that garden design and garden ornament in the Western world until comparatively recent times universally followed the classical tradition—the overwhelming stream flowing through Greece, Rome and Italy. The Gothic style and manner of thought scarcely enters into our theme until the landscape school triumphed, and then only in the form of pastiche. The small enclosed monastic and medieval gardens have little place in the account of subsequent garden design.

As a consequence, until the nineteenth century the formal gardens of cool northern Europe—and even the informal landscapes—are (with a few aberrant exceptions such as chinoiserie) predominantly decorated and ornamented in a manner evolved in and appropriate to the sun of the Mediterranean. Even today, much of the commercial work is still based on rather enfeebled versions of the great antique.

The English garden was not of much account until about the time when the influence of the Renaissance reached our shores in the Tudor period. At

Hampton Court, Wolsey's innovation in the new manner, the principal ornaments after its seizure by Henry VIII were '159 of the King's and Queen's beasts' carved in timber at '20s. the piece'. These were gilded and painted, set upon poles which were also gaily painted; on some were hung the King's, on others the Queen's, arms. There were also beasts carved in stone. This gay menagerie consisted of harts, lions, greyhounds, hinds, dragons, bulls, antelopes, griffins, leopards, yales, rams, tigers and badgers. The other principal ornamentation—if such it can be called—consisted of numerous 'brazen dials', which, as they were supplied by a clockmaker, must have been sundials. (The sundial, in a great variety of forms, was long a regular object of garden ornament—to be revived with some sentimentality in late Victorian days.) With the gaily painted rails around the flower beds, the scene was certainly bright and cheerful, if scarcely comparable with the contemporaneous Villa d'Este or with the French gardens designed by du Cerceau a decade or two later.

In 1598 the traveller Hentzner described the ornaments at the Burleighs' palace-like house at Theobalds. He wrote of

columns and pyramids of wood, up and down the garden; after seeing these, we were led into the summer-house, in the lower part of which, built semi-circularly, are the twelve Roman emperors in white marble, and a table of touchstone; the upper part of it is set round with the cisterns of lead, into which the water is conveyed through pipes, so that fish may be kept in them and in summer time they are very convenient for bathing.

Throughout the succeeding decades, British garden art came increasingly under the influence of the French and, towards the end of the seventeenth century, the Dutch. At this time Jan van Nost of Mechlen settled in England. With a large staff of assistants, he produced a great quantity of ornamental vases and other statuary between about 1686 and 1729. The work of his factory, of the highest quality, is inseparable from the gardens of London and Wise in the period of formal and ordered design that followed the accession of William and Mary, and which began to be superseded only after the death of Queen Anne. Fortunately much of this work remains, though the gardens (with an occasional exception such as Melbourne in Derbyshire), and the topiary which was their other ornamentation, have been destroyed. Thenceforth, with the coming of the landscape movement, the British hid their ornaments. (A late eighteenth-century painting of Powis Castle shows the terraces, now so richly laden with statuary contemporary with the period of their construction, quite naked.)

In France, however, and in those countries still under the domination of Le Nôtre, statuary and ornament continued in the classical manner, some of it particularly fine in quality: notable, for example, was the work of Lorenzo Matielli at the Schwarzenberg Palace.

At the end of the eighteenth century, with the rise of the romantically picturesque in taste and the sentimental in feeling, a great variety of ornament came into fashion. Coad and other artificial stones were used, followed by cast-iron. The design was often imitative, based on classic models, and the goods so produced were reasonable in price. Fountains, urns and a variety of ornaments and finials in every style were produced, often excellently designed; those manufactured by Felix Austin from 1828 onwards were particularly successful, and are not infrequently found today. The most distinctive Victorian garden feature was the cast-iron bench. The caster's sand was particularly sensitive to the pattern-maker's fronds of fern and acanthus foliage. The Coalbrookdale foundry was one of those prominent in the manufacture of such benches from about 1858. The Victorians, however, pressed everything into their garden design—even prehistoric monsters at the Crystal Palace.

In the era of William Robinson, Miss Jekyll and Lutyens, with its emphasis on the native tradition, obsolescent objects concerned with country crafts came into vogue—a notable example being the mushroom-like staddle stone upon which ricks were built. At about this time too—in the first decades of the nineteenth century—came the vogue for Japanese gardens. Even now, when the gardens themselves have disappeared, the heavy stone lanterns, birds and other pleasing paraphernalia connected with them still exist.

And finally, in the last few years, exhibitions in municipal parks (of all incongruities!) of extremely varied styles meaninglessly lumped together as 'contemporary'—both sculpture with human attributes (such as that of Henry Moore) and less representational works (such as those of Barbara Hepworth), as well as the new ranges of ceramic vase-like objects—have brought the brave new world into our gardens to compete with the more popular, and much less expensive, concrete bird-baths and plastic gnomes.

One point emerges from the present anarchy of styles. This is the thoughtful and imaginative use not only of the many new materials now available, but of both the old conventional kinds and of the equally old but unconventional. Indeed the material often dictates to the artist the form that his work should take. Further, the placing of the objects for display, and the design of surroundings for them, are usually considered and carried out with great imagination.

1 Statuary, Sculpture, Carved Figures in General

There are perhaps few features—water apart—which have been more important in the creation of buildings and gardens than sculpture. To see the colonnades of St Peter's in Rome at dusk with its myriad statues atop Bernini's great elliptical frame is awe-inspiring. To come across van Nost's lead figures in the glades of Rousham in Oxfordshire is equally significant, causing one to forget all the bad sculpture and even to find a temporary place in the affection for aldermen in stone 'retired' to local parks. At Burton Agnes in Yorkshire the surroundings of this late Elizabethan house have in recent years been enhanced by cleverly sited statues (plates 1 and 10). Anyone who also has walked along the broad walks at Versailles, Castle Howard or Chatsworth, with their lake fountains throwing white spumes high in blue skies, can again appreciate how great gardens are enhanced by carefully sited statuary. Those in the water garden at Versailles by Le Hongre show a leaning to classical art, and a cool stability that is quite distinctive.

In the sixteenth century particularly, but in other periods also, the sculptor's art often achieved its highest expression in equestrian figures. Bernini wanted his equestrian statue of Louis XIV at Versailles to lead the eye upwards, and the horse is rearing and pawing the air; however, after a remodelling by Giradon it became, instead of Louis XIV, a representation of Marcus Curtius plunging into a fiery abyss. In Ireland, at Powerscourt, there are bronze German horses of the 1860s superbly poised by the lake (plate 29). In England the horses are perhaps a little more placid, far removed from baroque sensibilities and requirements; such are the mounts that William III sits astride at Bristol, George I rides on the green lawns of Birmingham University's Barber Institute, and on which King John Sobieski of Poland sits, just outside the garden at Newby Hall in Yorkshire (plate 2). This last has a fascinating history. At one time Sobieski stood in London, having been erected there in 1672 by Sir Robert Vyner. The statue, of Carrara marble, is supposed to represent Sobieski as King of Poland trampling on a Turk, and to have been intended for erection in Warsaw. It was bought by Vyner at Leghorn, and when it was erected in London the head was changed to represent Charles II, the vanquished figure then symbolizing Cromwell. When the Mansion House was to be built the statue was removed in 1737 and taken to Lincolnshire, to be erected in Sir Robert's park at Gautby. It was not until 1885, after Sir Robert's descendant had inherited Newby, that it came to its present, unlikely position.

Few statues have such a story as this, but wherever they are—and there are many full-length frozen marble ladies at Newby, not far from Sobieski, set in alcoves in the long-walk hedges—they always add to the situation. The element of surprise as they are espied at the end of a vista, or the feeling of period given by a classical figure in Roman costume against a thick barrier of evergreens, is successfully achieved by few other means.

It was, therefore, natural that the creators of eighteenth-century gardens should turn to the lead figures of Jan van Nost, and later of John Cheere (plates 15 and 16), to supply their needs. In 1772 Cheere's place of business near Green Park in London was described as full of 'numberless figures in stone, lead and plaster . . . spruce squires, haymakers with rakes in their hands, shepherds and shepherdesses, bagpipers and pipers and fiddlers, Dutch skippers and English sailors. . . .' The repetitive nature of lead figures, however, caused those with the connoisseur's eye to turn to the great sculptors such as Rysbrack or Scheemakers (plates 14 and 38), and abroad to Bernini. The largest commission for decorative garden sculpture which Rysbrack received was from Lord Cobham, for his gardens at Stowe. Gibbs, Kent, Rysbrack and Scheemakers all worked to create the Italianate character of these gardens, and there is little doubt that it was Rysbrack himself who did the busts in the Temple of British Worthies.

If the eighteenth century found pleasure in the creation of works of sculpture for the garden, the nineteenth found as much pleasure in introducing a note of distinguished absurdity. The two nose-diving dolphins supporting a lamp-post in the gardens of Cliffe Castle at Keighley are perhaps the most accurate representation of a mill-owner's baroque that one could find. It is an engaging trifle, and at the other end of the see-saw, grossly out-weighing it, one could put the Albert Memorial with its panoply of mosaic and pious marble sentiment. Dr Johnson, with bowed head in the centre of Lichfield, looks as if he yearns to be in a garden; but William Pitt, in the gardens of Hanover Square in London, surely stands as if in mind of the dispatch-box of the House, scroll in hand and with tilted arrogant head.

While the rise in costs and the need for ease in maintenance have tended of recent years to curb the growth of great gardens, the garden siting of sculpture by contemporary sculptors seems to be on the increase. Of these modern examples, perhaps that with the most nonchalant sun-drenched air is the sculpture of the two maidens dressing their hair in the gardens of the Presidential Palace at Brasilia (plate 67). In England Henry Moore probably scores numerically; among many sites, those at Alderbourne in Buckinghamshire, at Edinburgh in the gardens of the Gallery of Modern Art overlooking the city (plate 46), and the sitings on grouse moors where the great sculptures stand four-square or four-holed to the winds, are most memorable. Those who have seen the figures by Barbara Hepworth set against sky and sea at St Ives in Cornwall (plate 43) will understand the international yearning to own a figure and to site it superbly. The Government of Victoria, Australia, has recognized the gifts of a sculptor in declaring a sculptor's gallery a national park. This is William Ricketts's mountain gallery, twenty-five miles from Melbourne, where fact mingles with fantasy in the remarkable sculptures of bush and aboriginal spirit figures (plate 68). The work is arranged in natural bush surroundings among tree-ferns and mossy rocks, on banks of native grasses and flowers, and in unexpected nooks and crannies.

The equestrian theme is not often attempted by contemporary sculptors. 'Riders of the Dawn' by Adolph Weinman is one of many fine pieces which adorn Brookgreen Gardens, near Myrtle Beach in South Carolina; two horses with riders rise on a great baroque plinth from a pool (plate 57). In contrast Willi Soukop's bronze statue of a donkey at Dartington Hall in Devon looks placid, ready to accept the burden of a gay child or a magpie paused in flight. It is ready to give pleasure and is thus representative of that indefinable quality of which gardens are the repository. Swallows skimming the water and sunlight glinting on marble to dissolve in a myriad hues are but part of the story: in sculpture we come near to the fullest realization of that which is most worth appreciation.

1 'The Gardener', an eighteenth-century lead figure in the garden at Burton Agnes, Yorkshire. In the background is a 'ha-ha'.

2 Equestrian statue of King John Sobieski of Poland, at Newby Hall, Yorkshire, originally erected in London in 1672.

3 Priapus, the god of garden fertility, Bodnant, Denbighshire.

4 'The Shepherd and his Dog', outside the gatehouse at Charlecote Park, Warwickshire, where Shakespeare is said to have poached in his youth.

5 Figures, in lead, of dancing shepherds and shepherdesses, on the balustrade above the orangery, at Powis Castle, Montgomeryshire.

6 'The Green Man of Peele', a rare eighteenth-century figure in a garden in Somerset.

7 Perseus holding up the head of Medusa, Melbourne Hall, Derbyshire.

8 Classical figures in lead, in the Botanic Gardens, Torquay, Devon.

9 'Diana the Huntress', Hinton Ampner House, Hampshire.

10 Hermes in the garden at Burton Agnes, Yorkshire.

11 Pan in front of the orangery at Powis Castle, Montgomeryshire.

12 Pan, Schloss Schwetzingen, Baden,
West Germany.

13 Satyr, in lead, playing a tambourine,
Tennessee Botanical Gardens, Cheekwood,
Nashville, Tennessee, U.S.A.

14 Rousham, Oxfordshire: 'A Dying Gaul', by Peter Scheemakers, after the original in the Capitoline Museum, Rome. In the eighteenth-century landscape garden by William Kent.

15 'The Nymph of the Grot', by John Cheere, in the Grotto at Stourhead, Wiltshire.

16 John Cheere's 'River God' in the Grotto at Stourhead.

17 One of the many statues at the Château de Versailles, Seine-et-Oise, France.

18 From the top terrace in the gardens of the Villa Garzoni, Tuscany, Italy.

19 Longleat, Wiltshire: the statue of 'Sir'
Jeffery Hudson (1619–82), a dwarf in
the service of King Charles I and Queen
Henrietta Maria, to whom he was first
presented at a banquet, served in a pie.

20 Figure in a garden in Kent.

21 Figure in the gardens of Schloss
Nymphenburg, Munich, West Germany.

22 'Quarrelling Cupids', Melbourne Hall,
Derbyshire.

23 Hermes in the grounds of Schloss
Nymphenburg, Munich.

24 Statue in the garden of Rechberg House, Zürich, Switzerland.

25 Figure by one wing of the Green Theatre, Bodnant, Denbighshire.

26 One of a pair of 'musicians' at Sandling Park, Kent.

27

28

27 Statues of Roman emperors from Hadrian's Villa, near Tivoli in Italy, with capped urns and other ornaments, in the exedra at Chiswick House, Middlesex, created by William Kent.

28 The walk with Hermae and other figures at Chatsworth, Derbyshire.

29 Pegasus in bronze, dating from the 1860s, at Powerscourt, Enniskerry, County Wicklow, Eire.

30 Hindu figure below the terrace at Lindridge Park, Devon.

31 Late eighteenth-century wooden sculpture of Winter in the garden of Billerud, Eastern Norway.

32 'Fame mounted upon Pegasus', in the forecourt at Powis Castle, Montgomeryshire. The group is all that remains of the Dutch-style water garden on a lower level.

33 Displaying peacock in lead, Powis Castle, Montgomeryshire.

34 Lead chanticleer, Tennessee Botanical Gardens, Nashville, U.S.A.

35 'Les Loups' (one of two) at one end of the Cascadette at the Château de Courances, Seine-et-Oise, France.

36 Dragon in a garden in Kent.

37 One of a pair of beasts (possibly monitors) at Knightshayes Court, Devon.

38 'Lion attacking a Horse' by Peter Scheemakers (after the original in the Capitoline Museum, Rome), Rousham, Oxfordshire.

39 Seated sphinx at La Belvedere, Versailles, France.

40 Seated sphinx, of a quite different pattern, in the grounds of Schloss Nymphenburg, Munich, West Germany.

41 Sphinx on the top terrace at Bodnant, Denbighshire, gazing wide-eyed over the surrounding countryside.

42 A pair of Egyptian sphinxes in the Victorian Egyptian garden designed by James Bateman at Biddulph Grange, Staffordshire, now an orthopaedic hospital.

43 'Archæan Figure' by Barbara Hepworth.

44 'Curved Form' in bronze, by Barbara Hepworth.

45 Barbara Hepworth's 'Cantate Domino'.

46 'Reclining Figures' by Henry Moore, Scottish National Gallery of Modern Art, Royal Botanic Gardens, Edinburgh.

47 Henry Moore's 'Reclining Figure', Dartington Hall, Devon.

48 Henry Moore's 'Draped Torso', Sparkford Hall, Somerset.

49 'Motif No. 3' by Henry Moore, in the
Water Gardens, Harlow New Town,
Hertfordshire.

50 Sculpture by Gerhard Marcks in a garden in Cologne, designed by Professor Hermann Mattern.

51 Sculpture by A. Ceschiatti in a garden in Brazil, designed by Roberto Burle Marx.

52 'Assia' by Charles Despiau, in the grounds of A/S Freia, Oslo.

53 A/S Freia, Oslo, the view from the garden pool: in the foreground 'Aklejaderna' by Eric Grate; in the background 'La Lune' by Henri Laurens. A/S Freia is a chocolate factory; these two examples show how modern sculpture may be used in the grounds surrounding industrial buildings.

54 Sculpture by John Skelton in a Sussex garden.

55 Bronze by Reg Butler in the Scottish National Gallery of Modern Art, Royal Botanic Gardens, Edinburgh.

56 'Cavaliere Babele' by Marino Marini, Sparkford Hall, Somerset.

57 'Riders of the Dawn' by Adolph Alexander Weinman, one of the many pieces of sculpture, traditional and modern, in Brookgreen Gardens, near Myrtle Beach, South Carolina, U.S.A.

58 Abstract bronze by Isamu Noguchi, its spiral shape symbolizing heredity, in the courtyard at the headquarters of International Business Machines Corporation, Armonk, New York, U.S.A.

59 Sculpture by Carel N. Visser,
Keukenhof, Lisse, Netherlands.

60 'Rest' by Gustave Kulche, Keukenhof,
Netherlands.

61 Sculpture by Kolbe in a garden designed by Professor Hermann Mattern of Berlin.

62 Bronze 'Bather' by Jacques Lipchitz.

63 'Family Group' by E. Bainbridge Copnall, carved direct from the trunk of an oak; photographed in the sculptor's garden in Kent, but now in a public concourse at Dudley, Worcestershire.

64 Sculpture by Hermann Haller in a public garden in Zürich, Switzerland.

65 Hermann Hubacher's 'Seated Girl' in a Zürich park.

66 Sculpture by Charles-Otto Bänninger in a Zürich park.

67 Sculpture of two maidens dressing their hair, by A. Ceschiatti, in the lake in the grounds of the Presidential Palace, Brasilia.

68 Aboriginal spirit figures in William Ricketts's mountain gallery, near Melbourne, Australia, now a National Park.

69 'Lochofant' by Otto Baum, in a large park-like garden.

70 Sculpture by Henri Laurens in a garden in St Hilaire designed by Professor Hermann Mattern of Berlin.

71 Sculpture by Hans Arp in a garden designed by Professor Mattern.

72 One of the 'gargoyles' in the Water Gardens, Harlow New Town, Hertfordshire, designed by William Mitchell, 1963.

73 'Torso of Adam II', in walnut, by John Skelton, in the grounds of the University of Sussex.

74 'Salome', in Hoptonwood stone, by John Skelton.

75 Life-size figures in *ciment fondu*, by T. B. Huxley Jones, in an Essex garden.

2 Water: Fountains, Fountain-Figures, Well-Heads, Canals, Ponds

Water, as has been said by more than one writer, is the soul of a garden. The aesthetically minded less frequently refer to the fact that water is the most essential material requirement to enable a garden to exist. There is a third point to consider: deep in the human system is a powerful desire to play with water. Who has not watched urchins making dams with mud in street-side gutters after a thunderstorm, and then breaking them and cheering the flush of water? And where is the adult who can stand by without emotion while Paxton's Emperor Fountain at Chatsworth (plate 78) is being turned on, and the jet gradually climbs up to its 267-foot apex above the lime trees?

The origin of all these 'water-works' (as they were called until the name became associated with municipal undertakings) was undoubtedly the canal that carried essential supplies of water in hot countries. The gardens of the East are planned round a rectangular network of irrigation channels. In the ruins of Pompeii the original narrow watercourses can still be seen today; they form a feature of the design, and as such were to be developed architecturally in the formal gardens of Europe, even where the sun shone but little and rain was abundant.

A fountain was originally no more than a source of water supply, not the piece of hydraulic engineering which we now consider it to be. Thus that most famous fountain of the ancients, Hippocrene, near Mount Helicon (and therefore sacred to the Muses), began as a simple gush of water from a patch of ground that had been struck, so it was said, by the hooves of the winged horse Pegasus.

The fountain was, therefore, the source of supply to the canal meshwork in the classical gardens. Thus Homer described the system in the garden of Alcinous (reputedly on Corfu):

Two plenteous fountains the whole prospect crown'd;
This through the garden leads its streams around,
Visits each plant, and waters all the ground:
While that in pipes beneath the palace flows,
And thence its current on the town bestows;
To various use their various streams they bring,
The People one, and one supplies the King.

46

By 1580, when Montaigne was in Augsburg, the system had developed:

We saw a big channel of water flowing to the town gate . . . this water is conveyed from outside the town by a wooden aqueduct. This channel of water sets in motion certain very numerous wheels which work several pumps, and by two lead channels these raise the water of a spring, which at this point is very low, to the top of a tower at least fifty feet high. Here the water pours into a big stone vessel, and from this vessel it comes down through many conduits, and from these is distributed throughout the town, which by this means is all crowded by fountains. Individuals who want a rivulet for themselves are allowed it on a payment of ten florins of rent a year. . . .

It is not surprising that when Montaigne reached Italy he found amazing developments of this comparatively simple, but to him surprising, piece of hydraulic engineering. The compatriots of Leonardo da Vinci, with their typical but astonishing combination of scientific research, aesthetic sensibility and mere gadgetry, had constructed fountains which produced music; concealed fountains that the gardener might turn on from a distance, so that the water sprang up unexpectedly from under one's feet; and also masterpieces such as that at Castello,

with two very big bronze effigies, of which the lower holds the other in his arms and is squeezing him with all his might; the other half fainting, his head thrown back, seems to spurt this water forcibly out of his mouth; and it shoots out with such power that the stream of water rises thirty-seven fathoms above the height of these figures, which are at least twenty feet high.

The subsequent history of the fountain, which culminated hydraulically, if not altogether aesthetically, in the French seventeenth-century formal garden, and today concludes with the little (and delightful) electrically operated squirt in thousands of suburban gardens, covers every style of ornamental architecture except that associated with the landscape period, when it was said that *jets d'eau* 'surprise by their novelty and the surprise is proportioned to the height to which they throw the water, but these columns of water have no pretence to beauty'.

Today, particularly on the continents of both Europe and America, we see some pleasing new designs breaking away from accepted practice and, as with sculpture, drawing particular attention to the inherent qualities of the materials used and their constructive capabilities. These hold promise for the future.

The canal is the contrast to the almost neurasthenic vitality of the fountain. Its placid calm is literally reflective, with no rainbow gaiety. Its effectiveness is dependent upon proportion, and it is surely seen at its best in the gardens of the seventeenth and early eighteenth centuries, and then particularly in the flatter landscapes. It was combined with a variety of geometrically shaped ponds, from the circular to much more complex patterns, at the centres of which was usually a fountain. The whole essence of a canal garden is that it should be regular and symmetrical; though a little liveliness may be brought to it by the construction of cataracts to move the water from one level to another.

Water gardens were made on a vast scale in France and those countries under French influence, where sometimes acres of water were used to produce the quintessence of calm horizontality. Contrasted with this, besides the fountains and cataracts, were the *gerbes d'eau, bouillons, goulettes, zic-zacs* and other ingenious contrivances designed to make water apparently perform against all natural laws—but these were only incidents in the total grand scheme. In Holland the canal gardens were on a smaller scale, much simpler and more intimate. Many of these European water gardens still remain, as do their more simple predecessors as, for example, in Spain and India. In the British Isles few survived the vogue for landscaping and irregularity that swept away the classic manner. Studley Royal, Yorkshire (plate 381), Westbury-on-Severn, Gloucestershire, a fraction of the Ebberston garden, something at Melbourne in Derbyshire, relics (the great cataract) at Chatsworth (plates 76 and 77), are about all we can show. Some British recompense for the destruction has been made by the Lutyens garden at New Delhi—on the grand scale—and by other smaller gardens Lutyens designed, such as Ashby St Ledgers; also by Harold Peto in his long canal garden at Buscot Park (plate 103). All these belong to the first decades of the present century.

Though the British swept away the formal water garden, they produced something in its stead which has not been surpassed elsewhere. When Nature came into fashion, and the straight banks of our regular canals were dug up and serpentined, every British landowner felt it incumbent on him to have his landscaped ornamental water. All the pundits who wrote on taste during the eighteenth century, and well on into the nineteenth, enlarged copiously on the designing of these 'natural' lakes. One of the most influential and widely read, Thomas Whately, devoted many pages of his study of gardens (*Observations on Modern Gardening*, London, 1770) to a section entitled *Of Water* which begins with a chapter on 'The Effects and Species of Water'. The result today is that many of our gardens are adjoined by lakes and large pools which, though they look natural enough, are not only man made but most artfully and carefully designed. They range from the Serpentine in Kensington Gardens (a series of more or less rectangular pools linked together at the behest of Queen Caroline in 1731), through the lake at Blenheim Palace, Woodstock (a giant magnification of the insignificant River Glyme) (plate 430), to Virginia Water in Surrey which, with the help of a bad flood in 1768, became, it is said, the largest sheet of purely ornamental water in the British Isles.

The principles underlying these large schemes have been—and are still—followed in the tiniest garden. Whereas the landscapers decorated their margins with trees, the miniature-scale landscaper of today uses choice water plants; probably, too, he takes a few suggestions from the Japanese water garden, which he so often sees illustrated.

A feature of old English gardens which is now frequently treated ornamentally is the moat. These, entire, or now existing only in part as ponds, are sometimes found encircling the manor-houses in those counties which have a high water-table. Many examples, for instance, are found in Warwickshire and Suffolk. Some have had charming bridges thrown over them; others, going back to an earlier age, have so-called 'fishing houses' decoratively placed on their banks.

In any discussion of water we must not forget the well—though it is now of very little practical importance, having undergone a vast change in status since piped water has spread over the country. The well-head, once so vital, was often a beautifully designed structure, so much so that in the days when such objects could be bought cheaply on the Continent many were imported, particularly from Italy, and on their merits alone—well or no well—used as garden ornaments (plates 109, 110 and 111). (By the same token, we may soon see the old disused village pump taking its place as an antique garden ornament.) When a well did exist it might even be housed, as at Melbourne, in a grotto-like building containing an appropriate exhortation:

Rest, weary stranger, in this shady cave
And taste if languid of the mineral wave.

We must accept the fact that tap-water is rather a come-down after the 'mineral wave', yet it can still give us pleasure in our gardens.

Finally, perhaps, a plea might be put in for the now ubiquitous swimming-pool. So often the private pool is a crude, utilitarian, mass-produced (or 'do-it-yourself') contraption set thoughtlessly in the middle of the lawn. Could this not be imaginatively designed, so that it too might achieve the status of a 'garden ornament'?

76 Chatsworth, Derbyshire, looking up the Cascade towards the Cascade Temple, built in 1703.

77 Chatsworth, the Cascade from the Cascade Temple. A plaque in the summer-house not far away bears the following lines:

'Won from the brow of yonder headlong hill,
Through grassy channels, see, the sparkling rill
O'er the chafed pebbles, in its murmuring flow
Sheds freshness on the thirsty vale below,
Quickning the ground till trees of every zone
In Chatsworths soil and clime, forget their own.'
            H. L. SEPT. MDCCCXXXIX

78 The Emperor Fountain at Chatsworth, designed between 1842 and 1843 by Joseph Paxton.

79 The calm circular pool, surrounded by architecturally clipped yew hedges, at Knightshayes Court, Devon.

80 The lake at Schloss Hellbrunn, Salzburg, Austria.

81 Reflections in the water: sculpture by Hermann Haller in a Zürich park.

82 The nineteenth-century formal Italianate pool with fountain at Bodnant, Denbighshire.

83

84

85

83 Dripping wall-fountain at Hidcote Manor, Gloucestershire.

84 Fountains in various classical forms at Schloss Hellbrunn, Salzburg, Austria.

85 In the lake at the Schwarzenberg Palace, Vienna, Austria (sculpture by Matielli).

86 'La Baigneuse' by Poivier, at the Château de Courances, Seine-et-Oise, France.

87 Versailles, the 'Bassin de Flora'.

88 Cascade and fountain, Schloss Linderhof, near Oberammergau, Bavaria, built for Ludwig II, King of Bavaria, in the 1870s.

89 Fountains in the park at Schloss Schwetzingen, Baden, West Germany.

90 (*below*) Multiple shell fountain at Schloss Nymphenburg, Munich, West Germany.

91 Classical fountain in the gardens of the Villa Garzoni, Tuscany, Italy.

92 The seventeenth-century Water Theatre at the Villa Aldobrandini, Frascati, Italy.

93 The fountain of the Muses and Pegasus, Villa Lante, Viterbo, Italy.

94 Classical fountain, Palace of Queluz, Portugal.

95 The Lions Fountain in the Court of the Lions, Alhambra, Spain, begun in 1377 by Mohammed V.

96 Formal pools and fountains at the Villa Taranto, Pallanza, Italy.

97 Granite swans, designed by Willi
Soukop in the 1930s, form a centrepiece
to a fountain at Dartington Hall, Devon.

98 A rectangular pool and three fountains,
in different kinds of granite, designed by
Eric Peskett in 1961.

99 Fountain in a garden in Stuttgart, designed by Professor Mattern of Berlin.

100 Fountain by Karl Selmert, with brick surround, in a garden designed by Professor Mattern.

101 Modern garden fountains designed by Gunter Neusel, with a surround by Professor Mattern.

102 Flower fountain, in cement, at a private house in Lahore, West Pakistan.

103 The water garden designed by Harold Peto at Buscot Park, Berkshire.

104 The early twentieth-century water garden at Blenheim Palace, Oxfordshire, with the Bernini fountains in the background and beyond them the eighteenth-century lake by Capability Brown.

105 The Shallimar Gardens, Lahore, West Pakistan, built by the Moghal Emperor Shahjehan in 1641. A view of the second terrace, from the first terrace. The third terrace can be seen in the background.

106 The ornamental water tank at Fronteira Palace, Portugal.

107 The water gardens in the Town Centre, Harlow New Town, Hertfordshire, designed by Harlow Development Design Group.

108 Water garden, designed by Susan Jellicoe, on the roof of Harvey's Store, Guildford, Surrey.

109 Italian well-head, Hodnet Hall, Shropshire. This was moved from Shavington Hall, near Market Drayton (now demolished) in about 1954.

110 Italian well-head with wrought-iron crane, the Dower House, Knowlton Park, Kent.

111 Italian carved stone well-head at Longwood Gardens, Pennsylvania, U.S.A.

112 Brick well-head in the gardens of Prentis House, Colonial Williamsburg, Virginia, U.S.A.

113 The fountain of Arethusa in the gardens of the Villa d'Este, Tivoli, Italy.

114 Loggia and Patio de la Acequia (Court of the Canal), Generalife ('Lofty garden'), Granada, Spain, built by Moorish sultans before 1319, when it was restored by the sultan Ismael.

115 Fountains and cascade in the Casino Garden, Villa Farnese, Caprarola, Italy. A Roman Renaissance garden.

116 Fountains, statuary, urns and finials in the garden of the Villa Lante, Bagnaia, Italy; another Roman Renaissance garden.

117 A view of the garden of the Villa Lante, showing the use of water and the parterres.

118 In the grounds of Hadrian's Villa, Tivoli, Italy.

119 Cascade, in the form of a crawfish (part of the arms of Cardinal Montalto) in the garden of the Villa Lante.

120 Fountains and pools, Villa d'Este, Tivoli, Italy.

121 The terrace of the hundred fountains, in the gardens of the Villa d'Este. A Roman Renaissance garden.

122 Pools, fountains and terraces in the seventeenth-century baroque garden of the Villa Garzoni, Collodi, Tuscany, Italy.

123 Formal pool with fountains in one of the hedged enclosures in the seventeenth-century garden of the Villa Marlia, near Lucca, Italy.

124 Fountain in a square pool, backed by a hedge of *arbor-vitae*, at Longwood Gardens, Kennett Square, Pennsylvania, U.S.A.

125 The water-lily pools, containing many varieties of tropical water-lilies and other aquatic plants, at Longwood Gardens. The main conservatory is in the background.

126 The Fountain Garden (1928–31) at Longwood, seen from the Conservatory Terrace. There are 229 jets, all of which can be illuminated in colour at night.

127 Fountains (1926–7) in the Open Air Theatre at Longwood.

128 In the Italian Water Garden at Longwood, constructed in 1925, based on the gardens of the Villa Gamberaia, near Florence.

129 The 'Eye of Water' at Longwood, inspired by the 'Fuente de Ojo de Agua' near San Antonio de Belen, Costa Rica.

130 The canal in the gardens of the Governor's Palace, Colonial Williamsburg, Virginia, U.S.A.

131 The baroque pebble and water garden at Dumbarton Oaks, Washington D.C., U.S.A. The pebble paving is kept constantly moist to accentuate the varied colours of the stones.

132 The lake at Powerscourt, Enniskerry, County Wicklow, Eire.

3 Vases, Urns, Pots, Cisterns, Troughs and other Containers

When one remembers that a 'container' can be a thumb-sized pot in earthenware to contain a small alpine plant, it is as well to think grand and visualize the great Waterloo Vase by Sir Richard Westmacott in the gardens of Buckingham Palace. This is fifteen feet high and bears a representation of part of the Parthenon frieze, a useful source of inspiration to many sculptors. The vase was begun in Milan at the order of Napoleon. It came to England unfinished, was decorated for George IV and was then given by William IV to the nation. Its great weight made it an unusual and undesirable exhibit in the National Gallery, and in 1906 it was offered to Edward VII. Its mass is now borne by the Palace lawns. The vases from Hadrian's villa at Tivoli are similarly far from home at Chiswick in Middlesex (*see* Plate 27).

Pride of place in any eighteenth-century garden, however, always went to the urns. These vase-shaped monuments to the dead, lying with open mouth or capped pineapple finial, are evocative, splendid in silhouette, and capture in one moment all that sense of proportion and adherence to classical principles which the age understood so well. Though Dr Johnson hated them, he was in the minority. The landscape gardener and poet William Shenstone counted it among his most important accomplishments that he was able to give advice to his friends about the erection and siting of urns. They allowed the display of learning by the inscription of long Latin epitaphs, they cost little, and sited—as Shenstone insisted—to be visible 'from every place, shrubbery, terrace, bowling-green, long walk and the end of the kitchen garden' could hardly fail to satisfy the contemporary demand for the morbid and the melancholic. If one could dash off Spenserian couplets or compose a Latin or Greek oration at demand, then an urn was necessary to display the achievement. Commemoration of the dead apart, few have stronger reason for existence than this—erected in mossy grot to be visited by the curious, or to be the meeting-place of the four long smooth walks around which such eighteenth-century gardens were always constructed.

Again, the lead cistern, originally made to collect rain-water, has often degenerated into a container for flowers. There is a dated example (1694) in the Deanery Garden at Exeter and another at the entrance to Burton Agnes in Yorkshire, but indeed they are often found and are to be associated, by the initials and heraldry they bear, with the family whose gardens they adorn. Burke said that 'Gardens are works of Art rather than of Nature', and it is certain that skill and ingenuity went into their adornment. Some of the containers from Italy at Iford Manor in Wiltshire seem carved out of great classical column-heads. What is certain is that fashions for certain plants led later to the production of decorative containers in which they could be planted —large handsome earthenware and terra-cotta pots, and the richly subtle Delft tulip pots with their glowing blue and white colours. By the early nineteenth century they were being made in artificial stone, and every Victorian azalea and fuchsia glowed in one in the hot conservatory, and every aspidistra glowered in a Burmantofts green bowl in the lace-bedecked parlour windows—outrivalled in popularity only by the 'monkey-puzzle' tree.

A return to the designs of the early lead containers has been made in recent times by the simulation of these classic shapes in glass-fibre. Costing a fraction of the price of the lead originals, and with as much claim to durability, these are a welcome innovation. It is to be hoped, however, that the patterns of the past will not remain the only inspiration of the creators of the glass-fibre garden container. Have they thought of asking a contemporary sculptor to design one? It should also be possible to exploit more adventurously the decorative possibilities in this field of colour-laminated aluminium sheets and wire meshes. Litter bins are already the subject of serious design, and most responsible local authorities can choose from a wide range when purchasing.

A brief chronological survey such as this, of features which are functional and yet were usually decorative, must inevitably, perhaps, end on this rather plebeian note. One ignores the humble stone pig-trough, which seems to have become a status symbol for plants in many a suburban garden and which, alas, was rarely decorated, and cannot help preferring the garden vase of classical design. Of good proportion, with poised cherubs or sphinx-like heads and a profusion of relief-masks of Roman emperors, it always looks right even without flowers. Indeed no sooner does it sprout the red geranium or orange nasturtium than the spells which storied urn and animated bust have cast fade away; it is then that, with Shenstone, 'I sigh, and grieve that I prize them no more'.

133 Elaborately sculpted capped urn on pedestal, Painshill, Surrey.

134 Lanhydrock, Cornwall. One of the bronze urns, modelled by Louis Ballin, goldsmith to Louis XIV, for the Château de Bagatelle.

135 Classical urn, Killerton Gardens, Devon.

136 Capped urn, with spiral design,
Petworth House, Sussex.

137 Capped urn, in lead probably mined
from the estate, at Powis Castle,
Montgomeryshire.

138 Stone urn of classical design, Tennessee Botanical Gardens, Nashville, U.S.A.

139–40 Urns of classical pattern in the gardens of the Governor's Palace, Colonial Williamsburg, Virginia, U.S.A.

141 Vases surmounted by eagles, at the entrance to Stourhead, Wiltshire.

142 The mid eighteenth-century urn above the Paradise Well, Stourhead, Wiltshire.

143 Plant container, Little EastonHall, Essex.

144 Vase of Regency 'basket-weave' pattern, at Powis Castle, Montgomeryshire.

145 Much-decorated vase at Hidcote Manor, Gloucestershire.

146 Vase supported by heraldic beasts (? lions rampant), at Sharpham House, Devon.

147 Capped urn, at the Schwarzenberg Palace, Vienna, Austria.

148 Plant-holder in front of ornamental crags in the small garden of the Forbidden City, Peking, China.

149 In the garden of the Katsura Detached Palace, Kyoto, Japan.

150 Capped urn, much eroded by the elements, in the garden of the Villa Garzoni, Tuscany, Italy.

151 In the grounds of Schloss
Nymphenburg, Munich, West Germany.

152 Cast-iron basket, probably Victorian,
in the garden at Hughenden Manor,
Buckinghamshire, once the home of
Benjamin Disraeli.

153 Orange trees in traditional tubs at Les Rochers, France.

154 Rustic vase decorated with oak leaves and boughs and a hunting scene, Portmeirion, Merionethshire.

155 Vase at Portmeirion.

156 Vase of eighteenth-century classical design in modern fibre-glass.

157 Orange trees in traditional tubs in the orangery at Saltram House, Devon, restored in recent years by the National Trust.

158 Terrace pots planted with pelargoniums at Northbourne Court, Kent.

159 Deep earthenware plant container decorated with swags of fruit, in a garden in Kent.

160 Shallow plant container planted with sempervivums at Sissinghurst Castle, Kent.

161 'Strawberry' pot planted with sempervivums.

162 'Patio' concrete plant bowl in white concrete, concrete paving and concrete bollards, all by the Mono Concrete Company Ltd.

163 'Chatsworth' flower box and hexagonal paving, both by the Mono Concrete Company Ltd.

164 'Kew' and 'Wisley' concrete plant bowls in a town setting.

165 Pre-cast concrete plant containers, used in conjunction with pre-cast concrete slabs and bricks in a Canterbury shopping concourse.

166 An hour-glass shaped asbestos-cement plant container in the Hansa Quarter, Berlin.

167 Stylized concrete plant container in a private garden in Lahore, West Pakistan.

168 Plant containers in a show-garden at Ane Park in Kassel, West Germany. Garden and containers designed by Professor Mattern.

169 A section of the trunk of a date palm, hollowed out and used as a plant container in a garden in Lahore, West Pakistan.

170 Various plant containers, garden furniture and the imaginative use of brick paving in the Texas garden of Mr and Mrs Arthur Berger.

4 Steps, Balustrades, Screens, Walls, Terraces, Obelisks and Finials

In the pot-pourri into which the reader may imagine he is to sink as we discuss seven different features of garden ornament, it is as well to strike out for some kind of order. But while, in an Alice-in-Wonderland world, it might be argued that, in order, one could ascend steps, pass balustrades and screens on walls and terraces, and espy afar off an obelisk with gilded finial, this would be an abstract ideal state, and in fact gardens are often better for disorder and asymmetry.

For obelisks, in England one would turn to Castle Howard, Yorkshire, with Vanbrugh's obelisk of 1714 to the third Earl of Carlisle (plate 196), or to that by Vanbrugh at Blenheim Palace in Oxfordshire. In 1714 Vanbrugh had sent the Duke of Marlborough 'a Draught of the obelisk my Lord Carlisle is raising', and his letters often mention obelisks small and great. Some are topped with balls and are to be 'scatter'd up and down the woods'. 'By this time an obelisk-addict', as David Green records in his book *Sarah, Duchess of Marlborough*, he explains to Carlisle: 'I keep to the Proportion of a Dorick Column which is eight diameters and that is the usual proportion of those in Italy, and succeeds mighty well into two pretty large ones in Mr Dodingtons Garden [at Eastbury in Essex].'

The long and complicated story of the Blenheim Column cannot be told here. Political and financial problems caused the project to be deferred to a time when neither the Duke nor Vanbrugh could be there in the flesh, and it was left to Nicholas Hawksmoor to propound the principles. The Grand Plinth was to be nine feet above the ground, 'to keep idle Persons from making Letters, and writing what stuff they please upon it, and doing other Mischiefs and Brutalitys'; upon the cornice at the foot of the shaft, space was to be found for the Roman Eagle and proper emblems as on the 'column of ye Emperour Trajan, one of the best of the Roman Emperours'. There was to be a noble inscription in Latin which Hawksmoor indicated 'ye Learned must direct'. For the star at the apex Hawksmoor turned again to classical authority. But all of this lay committed to his paper *Explanation* only. The obelisk finally became a column, topped by a statue of the Duke in Roman dress which was probably designed by Lord Herbert, and with a 'long . . . but very legible' inscription by Lord Bolingbroke—ironically the worst enemy of the irascible duchess, who had planned this monument over so long a period.

So the purpose of an obelisk is primarily to commemorate some event or person, whether it stands on the slopes of Hagley Park in Worcestershire (with a statue of Frederick, Prince of Wales atop), or whether it is the work of Bernini and stands in the Piazza Navona in Rome as the commemoration of a cosmic event—the gift of water distributed by great rivers to the four corners of the earth. A version of the latter obelisk (much approved, originally, by Hawksmoor) was finally set up at Blenheim in the 1760s, and in 1925 the 9th Duke of Marlborough incorporated it as an important feature of his Water Terrace Gardens (plate 104). Perhaps the noblest obelisk is not in a garden at all; that to Pope Sixtus V in Rome fulfils the Pope's own words that 'Rome does not only need divine protection and sacred and spiritual power, but also beauty which ensures convenience and worldly ornamentation'.

Some obelisks have finials, but this decorative ornament more often appears on pediments, gables, the apex of a roof or corners of a tower. It is also found on gate-piers, on urns and columns, and wherever the eye must be led over sturdy stone to a graceful finishing touch. It is carved to resemble a flaming torch or a pineapple, and in some instances, as at Montacute in Somerset (plate 175), it may even echo the form of the obelisk. In this example the finials surmount a balustrade, which is a row of balusters with a rail or coping forming an ornamental parapet or barrier.

At Cannon Hall in Yorkshire a stone balustrade acts as a barrier near a steep incline, and it echoes the parapet which the northern architect John Carr added to the seventeenth-century house in 1765. It is thus possible for the nicest of garden tricks to be played—for the eye to be led from balustrade to house and for a subtle interplay of light and style to occur, enhancing the whole.

The fine balustrades in Italian gardens have been copied in England, and that at Cliveden, Buckinghamshire, comes from the Villa Borghese in Rome and has sculptured water-basins, piers and recessed seats. The balustrade usually surmounts a low wall, but the wall itself often assumes a dominant role in compartmenting the garden and dividing the landscaped areas from those where the figs ripen and the apples hang on the outstretched arms of trees. Kitchen-garden walls of red hand-made brick encircle in dignified form many a garden. At Castle Howard in Yorkshire they are pierced by Samuel Carpenter's satyr-like mask piers and grotesque stone carvings (plate 216). Usually a dignified wrought-iron gate is a sufficient point of entry in a wall, but no feature announces a grand estate more readily than the long, nervous runaway length of a wall, flowing effortlessly along, seemingly for miles, until with a gradual ascent it flows upwards to grand piers, stone supporters and classical lodges at the entrance to a dukedom. Walls also house garden pavilions and bee-boles; sometimes they are 'warm-walls' to help in warding off frost from delicate fruit.

Perhaps, however, these features of wall, terrace, steps and balustrade come together most completely in Italian gardens, and possibly, too, at Powis Castle, Montgomeryshire, in Wales, where lead figures and topiary work enhance the steep descents (plate 5). Water also combines to beautify the setting of some of the French châteaux. At Vaux-le-Vicomte the architect

Le Vau knew how to combine the appearance of the house with demands for personal comfort and a suitable setting for entertainment. The principal front here is approached by broad flights of steps (Vanbrugh used similar dramatic effects at Castle Howard and Blenheim), and that other great French château, Versailles, with its water gardens and balustrades, bears witness not only to French civilization but to the greatness of Louis XIV.

It is always fascinating to look at the record of a garden over a long period, and at Longford Castle in Wiltshire we are able to do this from the period of Charles II onward. Engravings of that time show the balustrades decorated with ball ornaments, and the enclosures separated by high walls. Around all was a moat. According to an account of 1654 Lord Coleraine repaired damage done in the Civil Wars and 'new modelled the parterre, and with great cost first chalked then gravelled the walks, raising a terrace with a noble balister and rail of white ashlar all along the south side of the house'. As with many a formal seventeenth-century garden this was swept away by Capability Brown, but formality returned about 1840 with carpet-bedding and elaborately cut hedges. This was the style then in vogue, and in other parts of England Joseph Paxton and William Nesfield were working at great gardens such as Chatsworth, Harewood, Trentham and Shrubland Park to create geometric layouts.

The eighteenth-century garden at Longford had given due place to sculpture, and it is recorded that a certain William Privett of Chilmark (who also worked on many temples at Stourhead) was employed on the 'balustrade on ye walk', on an obelisk, and other sculptured features. . . . The nineteenth century turned to formality, but by 1950 it had become impossible to keep up this Victorian tradition. Trouble-free herbaceous perennials have now been introduced, and some gravel walks have been grassed; the raised and balustraded terraces remain. Freedom has been achieved within formality and a great garden still lives, with an infinite variety of colour and a greater ease in maintenance.

171 Herons in white-painted cast-iron in the garden at Arlington Court, Devon. There are similar finials on the gate-piers and there is a heronry in the grounds.

172 Finial at Eastwell Park, Kent; the crowned lion rampant bears the arms of Alfred, Duke of Edinburgh, Queen Victoria's second son. Note also the unusual arcaded balustrade.

173 Stone pineapple finial in a garden in Hereford. This is the true pineapple (*Ananas comosus*) as distinct from the fruit of the stone-pine (*Pinus pinea*) which is more often seen carved in stone to represent the so-called 'pineapple' finial.

174 Various finials at the Villa de Mattia, Asolo, Italy.

175 Balustrading, surmounted by 'obelisk' type finials, round the pool at Montacute, Somerset. Although these were made in the nineteenth century, they match those dating from Elizabethan times elsewhere in the garden.

176 Arcaded balustrading at Alton Towers, Staffordshire. Behind is the Choragic Monument, a memorial to the 15th Earl of Shrewsbury, based on the Athenian Temple of Lysicrates. In the background is the Chinese Gothic Temple.

176

177 Gate-pier finial in the Eagle Court, Tintinhull, Somerset.

178 Eighteenth-century pyramidal ball-topped finial at Castle Howard, Yorkshire.

179 The restored garden wall at Edzell Castle, Angus, originally built in 1604. Plants are grown in the cavities.

180 Screen, gates, various finials, a garden house and wooden seat of classical design in the gardens of the Governor's Palace, Colonial Williamsburg, Virginia, U.S.A.

179

180

181 Monoscreen walling by the Mono Concrete Company.

182 Screen wall in pre-cast concrete.

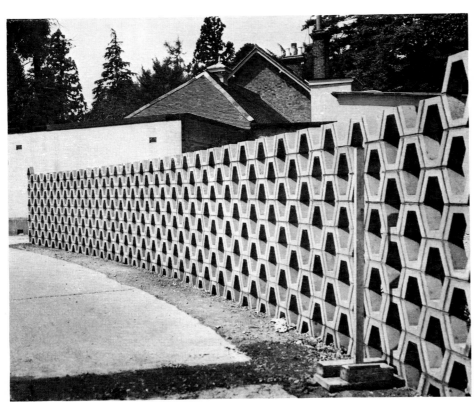

183 Flights of Elizabethan brick steps at Chilham Castle, Kent.

184 Curved steps and brick paving at Bodnant, Denbighshire.

185 Massive stone steps leading to 'Neptune', the Abbey Gardens, Tresco, Isles of Scilly.

186 Part of the grassed terraces overlooking the tournament ground at Dartington Hall, Devon.

187 Steps down to the Lotus Pool, Villa Taranto, Pallanza, Italy.

187

188

189

188 The Shell Fountain and steps at Dumbarton Oaks, Washington D.C., U.S.A.

190 Sphinxes flank the steps at Bodnant, Denbighshire. Note the unusual treillage pergola.

189 Balustrading of eighteenth-century pattern at Powis Castle, Montgomeryshire.

191 Walls, steps, balustrading and capped lead urns are all seen together at Powis Castle.

192 Steps, unusual finials, paving patterns and dripping fountains in the Casino garden at the Villa Farnese, Caprarola, Italy.

193 The Victorian terrace designed by Sir Charles Barry, at Shrubland Park, Suffolk.

194 The Fountain Terrace at Dumbarton Oaks, Washington D.C., U.S.A.

194

195 The Urn Terrace at Dumbarton Oaks.

196 The 100-foot obelisk at Castle Howard, Yorkshire. Designed by Sir John Vanbrugh for Charles Howard, 3rd Earl of Carlisle, it was erected in 1714 and stands at the intersection of two avenues. It was built to commemorate the planting of the plantations.

197 The Cobham Pillar at Stowe, Buckinghamshire, built in the mid eighteenth century. It is a 115-foot fluted column, surmounted by a domed cupola with a finial. The finial replaces the statue of Lord Cobham which was destroyed, together with part of the cupola, when the Pillar was struck by lightning in 1957.

5 Colonnades and Pergolas

To seek through Loudon's great *Encyclopaedia of Gardening* (London, 1822), in that fascinating section entitled *Permanent Horticultural Structures* (which covers everything from ice-houses to vegetable sculptures), for either colonnades or pergolas will be in vain. The nearest we come to them is in the discussion of espalier rails, which may be 'stakes driven into the ground 6 or 8 inches asunder' or cast-iron erections resembling common street railing. Again, one can go back to the writers on French formal gardens and still find nothing, which, in view of the Italian origins of that style of gardening, is surprising, for that great Italian, Alberti, wrote in his *Ten Books of Architecture* that 'the Ancients used to make their walks into a kind of arbours by means of vines supported by columns of marble of the Corinthian order, which were ten of their own diameter in height'. Surely, however, we shall find some information in the Victorian Shirley Hibberd's *Rustic Adornments for Homes of Taste* (London, 1857), for the modern rustic pergola provides the forester's great market for larch-thinnings; but not a word. Nor does Geoffrey Taylor mention it in *The Victorian Flower Garden*. Finally we end our search for historical information in the writings of that anti-formalist, Miss Gertrude Jekyll, and here we do find some explanation. At the beginning of the present century she remarked that it was surprising that although in the early days of gardening 'every kind of ornament and accessory' was introduced from Italy, it was only in recent years that the pergola had been adopted.

Indeed, even colonnades in the purely architectural sense, so common in classical architecture, are rarities—other than as rather elaborate porticoes—in our own classical buildings, though we do approach them in our medieval cloisters and the open-sided galleries of our early courtyard gardens.

At about the same time as Miss Jekyll was writing, the English garden architect, Thomas Mawson, observed that 'the steadily increasing love of fresh air and out-of-door life . . . makes a deep recess on the south front of the house almost a necessity'. As to pergolas, he goes so far as to say that they are essentials in a new garden to provide shade. And he refers to the use of unpeeled larch poles for pergolas in outlying parts of the grounds. His own designs are of substantial brick or stone pillars with stout oak cross-bars, or of massive carpenter's work. Both he and Miss Jekyll discuss suitable climbers to cover them. Presumably the difference between a colonnade and a pergola is that the former is primarily an architectural feature which may be embellished with plants, while a pergola is a structure built essentially for plants.

Miss Jekyll gives Harold Peto the honour of setting the example by designing pergolas 'of the highest expression of architectural refinement' in his work in the south of France. This example he and a number of other designers of varying merit followed in England. The vogue lasted until the beginning of the last war, but since then, presumably because of the high cost involved, it has lapsed. However, the good old rustic pergola, generally home-made and covered with rambler roses, still retains its crimson glory.

198 The arcade by the pool at Glan-y-Mawwdach, Merionethshire.

199 Part of the colonnaded forecourt at Antony House, Cornwall, completed in 1721.

200

201

200 A substantial stone and timber
pergola at Kewhurst Manor. The brick
and stone-on-edge paving is of unusual
pattern.

201 Stout timbers supported by classical
columns form the vine-clad pergola at
Chartwell, Kent.

202 The massive timber and masonry
pergola in the garden at Little
Thakenham, Sussex, designed by Gertrude
Jekyll early in the twentieth century
round the house designed by Sir Edwin
Lutyens.

203 Squared timbers are used for this
pergola in Kingsnorth Gardens,
Folkestone, Kent. Clothed with climbing
roses and clematis, it is altogether lighter
in construction.

204 Vine-covered arches in the gardens of Powis Castle, Montgomeryshire.

205 Pleached fruit pergola, flanked by sphinxes, Bowood, Wiltshire.

206 Pleached beech pergola or arbour in the formal gardens of the Governor's Palace, Colonial Williamsburg, Virginia, U.S.A.

207 The curved colonnades of Corinthian columns which form the entrance to Sans Souci, Potsdam, East Germany. The balustraded entablature is decorated with classical statuary and urns.

208 The massive wistaria-hung pergola at
the Villa Taranto, Pallanza, Italy.

6 Gates, Gate-Piers, Gate-Pier Finials

From the beginning gardens have had gates and gateways. The earliest surviving garden gates are wood, usually reinforced with iron; later, wooden framing was used with bars and sometimes cresting of iron. Iron gates were rarely used before the seventeenth century, though earlier examples are not unknown.

Of specimens of the older types, few retain even a part of the original structure; the wood in particular will have been repaired and replaced until nothing of the original remains. Some English examples are to be seen at Hampstead Marshall in Berkshire, Hutton-in-the-Forest in Cumberland and Groombridge Place in Kent (all wood with iron cresting); at Mapperton in Dorset (wood framework and panels, twisted iron bars) and at Eyam Hall in Derbyshire (wood).

Not all such gates are old, for wood may be preferred to iron, and indeed it is better to have a good gate of wood than an indifferent one of iron. Good wooden gates and fencing of nineteenth-century date may be seen at Hotvedt, Drammen in Norway (plate 220).

English gardens, up to the time of Elizabeth I and later, were usually walled (the idea came, through the Crusaders, partly from the East), and the gates leading into them were therefore often set in arched apertures and called 'planched' gates. There are specimens of such gateways at Tissington in Derbyshire (eighteenth-century, with a gate by Robert Bakewell), at Kirby Hall in Northamptonshire (seventeenth-century with rusticated stonework, possibly by Inigo Jones), at Greys Court in Oxfordshire (*c.* thirteenth-century) and at Castle Howard in Yorkshire (early eighteenth-century, by Sir John Vanbrugh) (plate 216). Larger gates were hung between stone or brick piers, to which we shall come shortly.

In these earlier gardens the idea was that the garden should be essentially an enclosure or 'garth', like the Béguinage at Bruges. It was not until the seventeenth century that the idea of a more open garden was conceived; then the whole landscape was included as part of the overall plan. For this, iron gates, strong enough to protect yet lacy enough not to impede the prospect, were needed. Celia Fiennes wrote (*c.* 1685–96) of a garden in which both aspects seem to have been incorporated. It was at the seat of Sir John St Barbe:

The Gardens are walled in, some with brest walls some higher with flower potts on them, severall places with open grates [claires-voies: see Chapter 8] to look through with stone balls or figures on the pillars each side the Gates every way . . . the Gardens are not finish'd but will be very fine with large gates open to the Grounds beyond some of which are planted with trees. . . .'

England is rich in fine examples of iron gates of the eighteenth century—our blacksmiths' golden age. Thomas Robinson, a follower of Tijou's (see Chapter 8), made the gate and screen, *c.* 1710, at New College, Oxford (plate 229), which stand between the college court and gardens, together one of the finest extant examples of English blacksmithery. Robert Davies's gates at Chirk Castle in Denbighshire, *c.* 1717 (plate 228), were one of the first architectural iron structures in England to incorporate cast-iron (for the caps on the piers). At Clare College, Cambridge, are gates by Warren, *c.* 1714, with laurel leaves in the centre of the overthrow so lifelike that they show even the fibres where they would have been torn from the branch.

Of later gates, the fine cast-iron set between Hyde Park and Kensington Gardens in London have cast-iron piers surmounted by finials of cherubs and crowns. They were originally made, by the Coalbrookdale Company, for the Crystal Palace Exhibition in 1851. A later set, a heavier and more stodgy combination of cast- and wrought-iron, is at Wimpole in Cambridgeshire.

Foreign specimens include pleasing gates in the courtyard of the Palazzo Bevilaqua, Bologna (*c.* 1500). The elaborate seventeenth-century gates at Versailles are monumental, heavily gilded and intimidating, as befits the residence of the Sun King. In contrast the delicate gates at the Villa Carlotta, Cadenabbia (*c.* 1745), a focal point at the base of the terraced gardens, seem as light as a cobweb. But Italian examples abound—in the Giardino dei Giusti in Verona, the Villa Foscari at Malcontenta, the Villa Manin at Passariano and the Ca' d'Oro in Venice where they open into the garden direct from the Canale Grande. But none has the elaboration of rococo iron gates in Austria, Hungary and Czechoslovakia, unless it is those of Jean Lamour in the Place Stanislas at Nancy (1755). For magnificent modern gates (and indeed for smithcraft in general) Germany has the best to offer. Most of it is, however, so far as our subject is concerned, in private gardens.

Fine gates need magnificent piers to set them off. And piers need finials to surmount them. Among the finest piers in Britain are those at Hampstead Marshall in Berkshire (seventeenth-century). Some are of sculptured stone, others of brick and stone. They are surmounted by finials: balls, vases and pineapples. The stone ones have sculptured panels of flowers, leaves, cornucopias and trophies. But those of stone and brick are more attractive, especially in the elevations with niches surmounted by stone cockle-shells. These were probably never intended to contain sculpture, but to give every advantage of light, shade and interest to the surfaces. Simpler stone piers with niches are at Boringdon in Devon; they are surmounted by enormous granite balls. Others, more elaborate, are at Mapperton in Dorset (seventeenth-century); they are surmounted by eagles. Wren's 'flower-pot' piers at Hampton Court, of carved Portland stone, have niches, and are surmounted by lead amorini by Jan van Nost bearing baskets of fruit and flowers.

Armorial charges are often used as finials, as at Staunton Harold in Leicestershire, where a greyhound and a stag support shields on curved pediments at the head of Corinthian 'barley-sugar' columns. The leaping horse of the Trevelyans may be seen at Nettlecombe Court in Somerset (plate 221).

The obelisk was a favourite finial in Jacobean times. A pair of these, of considerable elegance, surmount stone piers at Canons Ashby in Northamptonshire; others decorate a stone-wall gateway in the garden of almshouses at Oundle, and specimens are at Renishaw Hall in Sheffield and Bramshill in Hampshire. But the number of subjects used for finials seems infinite. A random list includes dragons, at Glynde in Sussex and Powis Castle, Montgomeryshire (plate 210); lions, at Hampton Court, at Kirkleatham Hall in Yorkshire and Eastwell Park, Kent (plate 172); stags, at Somerleyton Hall, Suffolk; vases, at Stibbington Hall, Huntingdonshire, and Barrow Court, Somerset; angels with trumpets, at Harrowden Hall, Northamptonshire; Bluecoat boys in lead, at Hertford; kneeling kings, at Grimston Court, Yorkshire; spiked balls, at Eaton Hall, Chester; eagles and vases, at Drayton House, Northamptonshire; eagles, at Bingham's Melcombe in Dorset, Tintinhull in Somerset (plate 177), and in the U.S.A. at Riverdale, New York; knapped flint pineapples, near Hilton in Dorset.

Elaborate piers, each consisting of four Ionic columns on bases, supporting entablatures which in turn support amorini and vases, are in the Garden of the Prince at Aranjuez, laid out by Charles IV when he was Prince of the Asturias (eighteenth-century). Large statues surmount the piers at Cadenabbia (see above), sphinxes and goats those at the Boboli Gardens in Florence (sixteenth-century), and double volutes at Bagheria in Palermo and Villa Vescovo at Lucca (both seventeenth-century). At the last, the piers have niches which contain statuary. At Vreedenhof in Holland are elegant baroque baluster-shaped piers.

An essay on garden gates and piers would be incomplete without at least a brief mention of the ubiquitous Japanese *torii* or Shintô gate—that distinctive arch-like erection to be seen in so many temple gardens in that country. It is a symbol, marking the entrance into the hallowed ground of a gateway or tomb. There are many forms. It is claimed that they should be made of wood, but some are made of other materials—stone, metal, porcelain, or even ferro-concrete. Particularly interesting specimens are at Kyoto (for instance in the Palace grounds), Sakamoto, Lake Biwa, and standing in the waters of the inland sea at Itsukushima Shrine.

Finally there are the circular moon gates of oriental origin, and sometimes used in Western gardens. A good specimen is in the Bagh-e-Jinnah Gardens at Lahore (plate 219).

209 Wrought-iron gate at Powis Castle, Montgomeryshire. The gate-pier finials are the heraldic beasts known as wyverns which had their origins in the fire-drake or dragon. Similar beasts, but with mouths agape, can be seen on gate-piers at Glynde Place, Sussex.

210 Wrought-iron gate at Packwood House, Warwickshire. The gate itself is simple in design, but swings between two elaborate side-panels. The overthrow, with its flower and foliage motifs in repoussé work, surmounted by a unicorn's head, is equally decorative. The niches with arched tops on each side of the gateway are bee-boles, in which the old straw bee-skeps were over-wintered.

211 Eighteenth-century wrought-iron gates and screen at Mellerstain House, Berwickshire. The decoration is mainly scroll-work.

212 Wrought-iron gates at Lindridge Park, Devon. The arrow-shaped dog-bars terminate at their bases with scrolls. The overthrow is unusual in that it has a curved stretcher which forms a perfect oval with the dip on the top of the gates.

213

214

213 The wrought-iron gates at Hinton Ampner House, Hampshire. They are strong in construction, the scrolls and bars adding strength as well as decoration.

215 Elaborate wrought-iron gates at Olantigh, Kent. Of unknown origin, they are decorated with motifs of fruit and flowers, masks, human figures and birds, as well as scroll-work. The top cresting has further floral decorations as well as heraldic shields and the motto 'Mort en Droit'.

215

214 A gateway of massive construction at Appletree Cottage, Brancaster, Norfolk. The gate is of simple design, the decoration consisting mainly of scrolls.

216 One of the gates to the walled garden at Castle Howard, Yorkshire, dating from the early eighteenth century. The best-known gate is the Satyr Gate, with masks of satyrs on the great piers instead of the lion masks shown here, though otherwise similar. The stone carvings were done by Samuel Carpenter.

216

217 Eighteenth-century wrought-iron gates and screens at Portway House, Warminster, Wiltshire, restored by Lucien Varwell. Their decoration appears to be in the 'Chinese Chippendale' style. The heraldic eagle is covered with separate leaves of copper, painted white, and its head and gilded gorget are of lead. The gate-piers carry unusually small gilded leaden balls to signify a manor house.

218 (*above*) A 'Moon' gate in the garden of Hill Pasture, Essex, a modern romantic landscape garden.

219 'Moon' gate in the Bagh-e-Jinnah Gardens (formerly known as Lawrence Gardens), Lahore, West Pakistan.

220 Wooden gates and fencing at Hotvedt, Drammen, Norway.

221 Gate-pier finial at Nettlecombe Court, Somerset. The leaping horse is the device of the Trevelyans.

222 Acorn gate-pier finial at Stanton
Harcourt, Oxfordshire.

223 Stylized 'pineapple' at Lower
Slaughter Manor House, Gloucestershire.

224 Wrought-iron gates to Westover
Plantation, Charles City County, Virginia,
U.S.A., probably made in the first half of
the eighteenth century for William E.
Byrd (whose initials are incorporated in
the ironwork), founder of Richmond,
Virginia. The lead eagle finials are a play
on the name Byrd.

225 Stone-pine cone finial with acanthus leaf decoration on the base, on a gate-pier at Tennessee Botanical Gardens, Cheekwood, Nashville, Tennessee, U.S.A.

226 The wrought-iron entrance gates to the Tennessee Botanical Gardens.

227 Wrought-iron gates in the gardens of the Governor's Palace, Colonial Williamsburg, Virginia, U.S.A.

228 The iron gates of Chirk Castle, Denbighshire, *c.* 1717, made by Robert Davies. The bases and certain other parts are made of cast-iron. The baroque design, incorporating numerous plant motifs, cockle shells, masks, gargoyles and scrolls, with fountains, birds and a coat of arms on the overthrow, is an amazing example of blacksmith's work.

229 The gate and part of the screen at New College, Oxford, made by Thomas Robinson *c.* 1710 and restored in recent years by George Lister & Sons Ltd. The design consists mainly of scrolls with a certain amount of repoussé work.

7 Sundials, Astrolabes, Armillary Spheres

The sundial, the most accurate timekeeper known to the Ancients, was mentioned in the Book of Isaiah (*c.* 700 B.C.): 'Behold, I will bring again the shadow of the degrees, which is gone down in the sun dial of Ahaz, ten degrees backward.' It has been used for some 3,000 years, perhaps for much longer if we include such devices as a pole stuck into the ground to mark, by the length of its shadow, the position of the sun in the sky and therefore the time. Stonehenge may have been in part related to timekeeping by shadows thrown by the sun; if so, the sundial's prehistory may be extended by at least 1,000 years before the time of Isaiah. It was known to the Babylonians, who passed it on to the Greeks, who passed it to the Romans. It was known also to the Arabs, who developed the science of sundial construction (gnomonics).

The two important parts of a sundial are its dial (graduated in hours) and style, a rigid bar whose shadow is thrown onto the dial to indicate the time. The dial may be fixed horizontally, vertically, or inclined to the horizon. The first is the commonest and is usually fitted to the top of a column. The others are usually fixed to walls, though not invariably, for they too are sometimes mounted on columns.

Because they need bright sunlight to function, a garden, and in particular one without high trees, is an ideal position for them, and so they have become accepted garden ornaments, even since the invention of clocks.

In past centuries sundials were used lavishly, as this extract from Henry VIII's Exchequer accounts shows: 'Also paid to Bryse Auguston, of Westminster, clockmaker, for making of 20 brazen dials for the King's new garden [i.e. Hampton Court] at 4s. 4d. the piece £4 6s. 8d.'

An ancient stone sundial—perhaps it is 1,000 years old—is in the grounds of the ruins at Monasterboice in Ireland, near the North Cross. But though such old sundials are interesting, they are decoratively primitive compared with such later magnificent examples as the vertical specimen (1733; it replaced an earlier dial of 1642) on the wall of Queen's College Library, Cambridge, brilliantly painted with the signs of the zodiac and with tables of calculations which include the number of hours and minutes to add when reading it by moonlight, for which it has a second style. Another, though simpler, specimen is on the wall of King's College Chapel, Cambridge. Modern specimens have been erected, somewhat unhappily, on the Gate of Honour at Gonville and Caius College.

A splendid vertical sundial with four dials is at Old Place, Lindfield, Sussex; another is at the Palace of the Quirinal in Rome (1718), and yet another in the garden of York Hall, Yorktown, Virginia, U.S.A. Others, on polyhedra, are at Heslington House, Yorkshire, and Barrington Court, Somerset (plate 230). Yet another, this time with two polyhedra, one above the other, is at Balcarres in Fife, Scotland. There are indeed many more fine sundials in Scottish than in English gardens. Others are at Drummond Castle in Crieff (1630; designed by John Mylne for the Earl of Perth), Glamis Castle in Angus (plate 232), Holyrood House in Edinburgh, and—one of the best of all—at Newbattle Abbey, Midlothian.

Fine horizontal dials are at Crathes Castle, Kincardineshire; the Fellows' Garden at Christ's College, Cambridge; Port Sunlight, near Birkenhead in Cheshire; the Bishop's Palace, Chichester, Sussex; Buen Retiro, Churriana, near Malaga (an elaborate and monumental example of the seventeenth century); Hickory Ground, Baltimore, Maryland; the Arsenal, Frankford, Pennsylvania (its pillar is an old cannon). One could continue giving examples for pages.

Charming features of many dials are their inscriptions, usually indicative of the transitoriness of life or the speedy passage of time. They may vary from a simple *tempus fugit* to whole verses, though these are scarcer. Many hundreds of such inscriptions were collected by Mrs Alfred Gatty and published in *The Book of Sun-dials* in 1888 (a third, enlarged edition was published in 1890).

The armillary sphere is a much more recent invention. It is constructed of rings, usually of brass (though other materials are known), representing the paths of certain bodies in the celestial sphere. The astrolabe, another more recent device, represents on a plane surface the apparent movement of the stars across the sky. The word was later applied to an instrument for taking latitudes at sea, but it is the former kind which is found in gardens, though even then but rarely, for the astrolabe is almost invariably a small hand-instrument. Larger ones do exist, however, such as the seven-foot instruments of iron and brass (eighteenth-century) in the grounds of Jai Singh's observatory at Jaipur, perhaps brought by him from Delhi. Astrolabes forming part of clocks are sometimes found, particularly on the Continent, but most of them are inside buildings. Fine outdoor specimens are at Prague and Ulm.

Sometimes armillary spheres formed part of sundials. One is in the gardens of Ashridge Park in Hertfordshire. In such instances the vertical axis of the sphere forms the style, and its equatorial ring is graduated into hours to receive the shadow. Another is at Kingston Lacy in Dorset, where there is also a fine old horizontal sundial.

One of the earliest surviving outdoor armillary spheres must be the Mongolian specimen, *c.* 1274, in the grounds of the Astronomical Observatory at Peking. It was made to the design of Ko-Shun-King, astronomer to Kublai Khan (1216–94). The sphere is of cast bronze, about 194 centimetres in diameter, and is supported by four bronze dragons. It is a true scientific instrument, with movable pivots and circles; yet it is astrological too, for on the inside of the horizon circle are inscribed, in Chinese, the names of the twelve states into which the old Chinese empire was divided, each being given that portion of the heavens thought to influence it. Near by is another even larger specimen 300 centimetres in diameter. It was made, in 1674, to the order of Père Ferdinand Verbiest (1623–88), surveyor and mathematician to the Chinese Emperor.

Less exotic examples may be seen in the Madeira Gardens, Brighton, Sussex; in the Wellington Pier Gardens, Great Yarmouth; in Sandford Orcas Manor, Dorset; in the grounds of Tryon Palace, New Bern, North Carolina (plate 237); and—on a grander scale—in the Italian Garden at Somerleyton Hall, Suffolk.

230 The ten-faced sundial at Barrington Court, Somerset.

231 Many-faceted sundial in the garden at Pitmedden, Aberdeenshire.

232 An early seventeenth-century sundial at Glamis Castle, Angus. The four lions rampant, derived from the arms of the Strathmore family, bear shields with dial faces; the names of the days and months are engraved below. The large block above is cut into eighty triangular planes into each of which a gnomon is fixed. The structure terminates in a coronet.

233 Combined sundial and direction finder at Bodnant, Denbighshire. The plinth was once the base of another sundial. On the metal disk below the sundial (which has two gnomons) are engraved the positions of farms on the Bodnant Estate and mountains in the Snowdonia range.

234 Sundial at Davenham, Worcestershire, mounted on the capital of a column of the Renaissance Composite Order.

235 Wall-mounted sundial at Levens Hall, Westmorland.

236 Armillary sphere at Tintinhull House, Somerset. The rings represent the great circles of the heavens and they are put together in their relative positions. The time is indicated by the shadow cast by the shaft which passes centrally through the sphere, terminating in the representation of the sun.

237 Armillary sphere mounted on a bell, in the grounds of Tryon Palace, New Bern, North Carolina, U.S.A.

238 An analemmatic sundial, Longwood Gardens, Pennsylvania, U.S.A. The dial is forty feet in diameter and is the largest of its kind in the world.

239 A simple sundial forms the centrepiece in this garden, laid out in the shape of a four-leaved clover, at the Palmer House, Colonial Williamsburg, Virginia, U.S.A.

8 Ironwork in the Garden

In general, ironwork is of two kinds—wrought and cast. Of these, wrought-ironwork may be subdivided into blacksmithery, in which the iron is shaped at red heat on an anvil; locksmithery, in which it is shaped cold; and repoussé, in which designs are raised on iron sheet by punching. Cast-iron is iron melted and poured into moulds.

Blacksmithery is the oldest method and has been known to man for millennia. Locksmithery's heyday was the Middle Ages; it was rarely, if ever, used for garden ironwork and will therefore not concern us here. Repoussé has been used on other metals for many centuries, but, armour apart, was not used on ironwork until the seventeenth century. Cast-iron is more recent and for garden ornament is essentially of the nineteenth century, though it is still used.

Early exterior ironwork is scarce. Rust has ravaged it and, generally speaking, the earliest specimens likely to be found in English gardens belong to the seventeenth century, and even these are scarce. Abroad, where the climate is somewhat kinder, earlier work still exists. Such are the many delightful window grilles overlooking gardens in Spain (such as Salamanca and Seville, sixteenth-century), or the elaborate well-head grille at Grafenegg Castle in Austria (c. 1570).

In England a golden age of wrought-ironwork was ushered in at the end of the seventeenth century by Jean Tijou, a Huguenot smith brought here by William and Mary. He worked for Wren at St Paul's Cathedral, and employed a staff from which sprang a fine school of blacksmiths.

Tijou's greatest contribution to garden ironwork was his stately Fountain Screen at Hampton Court in which, on great frames of scrollwork, are represented the badges of England, Scotland, Ireland and Wales, the garter and royal monograms, all amid a splendid display of repoussé leaves, crowns, birds, masks and other devices. Tijou was the greatest master of repoussé ever to work here. His other great contribution to garden ironwork, the screen at Wimpole, was swept away during eighteenth-century 'improvements'.

His followers included Robert Bakewell, who made the 'Birdcage' (c. 1710) in the gardens at Melbourne Hall, Derbyshire (plates 240 and 241), a truly poetic structure of scrollwork overlaid with masks, birds, flowers and leaves, and with crowning tendrils of oak and laurel; and Robert Davies of Croes Foel, who made the *claire-voie* at Leeswood Hall, Mold, Flintshire, which, with its broken pediments, diving dolphins and other details, echoes contemporary continental work. It is indeed fortunate that these works, and others by the same craftsmen, are still in their original settings.

At Trinity College, Cambridge, magnificent grilles (by Partridge, a London smith, *c.* 1678) fill in the arches of the colonnade beneath Wren's library overlooking the garden and river, giving the whole setting a shady, Venetian air. At Clare College, on either side of the garden drive, are modern (1963) wrought-iron lamp-posts, made by local craftsmen and designed to echo motifs from Warren's gates (see Chapter 6).

Italian gardens are noted for such excellent ironwork as the delicate scrolled eighteenth-century balustrade around the artificial lake at the Isolotto at Palazzo Pitti, Florence, on which one may lean to look across to a little island with lemon trees, while marble sea-horses rise from the water. And there is the eighteenth-century chinoiserie ironwork on Palazzina Cinese at Palermo, on a stairway into the garden.

Indeed, in past times hardly any great garden lacked ironwork. At Versailles there are railings resplendent in black and gold, interspersed with lyre motifs and suns in glory (seventeenth-century). At Malmaison simpler railings lead from the garden to Percier and Fontaine's wings, added in 1799. Elaborate rococo railings flank the garden stairway at Schönbrunn (eighteenth-century). In Holland, at the Huis ten Bosch, the garden stairs have elegant if simple design (seventeenth/eighteenth-century). More elaborate are the staircase railings on the garden stairs at Tullgarn, the Baltic lakeside residence of the Swedish royal family.

Of smaller objects, lamps and brackets are among the most pleasing. An elaborate specimen is in the garden of the house, 'La Begude', at Cagnes-sur-Mer; others are at Portmeirion, Merionethshire. A pleasant modern balustrade is in the garden of 'L'Oiseau Bleu' at Villefranche-sur-Mer.

In the nineteenth century cast-iron verandahs, screens and gates were widely used, especially in English spa towns such as Leamington, Cheltenham and Dawlish. Cast-iron railings and bollards may be seen everywhere. The metal acquires in time a pleasant texture contrasting well with that of stone, and acting as a foil to the foliage. It is combined with wrought-iron on pleasantly simple railings across the Pont du Béguinage in Bruges. Throughout the boulevards in Paris it is used for pavement grilles around the plane trees; smaller pavement grilles may be seen at Saffron Waldron in Essex. One of the richest towns in cast-ironwork is Brighton, Sussex; it may be seen there in thousands of variations. In the Pavilion Gardens are lamp-posts of *c.* 1835, with reeded bases and the crown and monogram of William IV. The fountain in the Old Steine Gardens is a *tour de force*. And the Madeira Gardens are set in a continuous framework of late nineteenth-century cast-iron on two or three levels.

Cast-iron vases, sundials, seats and statuary were popular throughout the nineteenth century. A splendid life-size group of a huntsman and hounds is in the gardens of Anglesey Abbey. Many 'standard' sculptures were reproduced in the metal, among them the Mercury of Giovanni de Bologna, a specimen of which, approximately half life-size, is in a private garden on Milton Road in Cambridge. Cast-iron seats and chairs are in public gardens everywhere and of varied patterns. Those in the Embankment Gardens at Westminster, for instance, have kneeling camels (nineteenth-century). Those in front of the Belgrade Theatre in Coventry have fantastic horses (1961). Cast-iron vases and urns are almost as common.

Glass-houses built on a cast-iron framework and containing cast-iron gratings and other embellishments form an important category of garden ironwork, much of it inspired by the example of the 1851 Crystal Palace, which was constructed on this principle. One of the finest specimens of this class of building is the Palm House at Kew (Decimus Burton and Richard Turner; begun 1844).

240 The great wrought-iron 'Birdcage' arbour at Melbourne Hall, Derbyshire, made in the eighteenth century by Robert Bakewell of Derby and restored in 1958 by George Lister & Sons Ltd.

241 Inside the arbour, looking up into the cupola and birdcage-like dome.

242 Wrought-iron balustrade decorated with leaves, fruits and tendrils of the grape vine as well as scrolls and twists.

243 Wrought-iron balustrade at Powerscourt, County Wicklow, Eire, decorated with flower and other motifs. Note also the fountains and the wall-mounted sundial.

244 A decorative metal archway at Portmeirion, Merionethshire.

244

245 Metal ornament at Portmeirion.

246 Decorative *claire-voie* at Portmeirion. The motifs are almost entirely nautical or marine.

247 Cast-iron sculpture in a garden at Skien, Norway.

9 Treillage and Trompe l'Œil

Briefly, the art of treillage (from Latin *trichila* and French *treille*—tendril or vine) consists of architectural design expressed through wooden lattice-work. At its most elaborate, as in the Temple d'Amour at Chantilly, it has the refinement of work conceived in more durable material such as stone or iron. In the words of a nineteenth-century architect:

Such a medium may be to the Architect what clay is to the Sculptor: in it he may venture to give shape to some poetic dream of ethereal architecture which has visited his brain. . . . It can be altered and shifted at pleasure until the desired effect is obtained in a way which more solid and valuable materials prohibit. . . .

Treillage and simple trellis-work, from which it stemmed, have been used as garden ornament for centuries. Frescoes discovered at Pompeii show elaborate trellis garden structures such as aviaries and summer-houses, though these early structures were made of entwined canes and reeds and not of flat wood strips like modern work. It was known, too, in the Far East and in Arab countries, where its elaborate form, *mashrabiyyah*, stood between the garden and the *zenana*. Medieval and later representations of treillage in paintings abound, as in a manuscript of the *Romaunt de la Rose* (British Museum), in the printed book *Poliphili Hypnerotomachia* (Aldus, Venice, 1499), and in Luini's 'Madonna of the Rose' (Brera Gallery, Milan). And there are later representations by Watteau, Fragonard, Lancret and others.

Indeed the greatest age and centre of treillage was eighteenth-century France, and it may be seen at its finest at Chantilly where it appears in many forms, though much of it is not original eighteenth-century work, for such light woodwork soon rots and has to be replaced. Simpler specimens are in many Paris gardens, as at 252 boulevard St Germain and 33 rue Faubourg St Honoré (Union Interalliée).

L'Art du Treillageur (Paris, 1745) gives many details of construction. Strips of ash, chestnut and oak were joined together at the intersections by iron wire, not by nails. Iron was used to strengthen the construction, and painted iron flowers and leaves were used to embellish it.

Treillage (Dutch *latwerk*) was used to decorate Dutch formal gardens. In England it has been used since the sixteenth century, though little early treillage remains here. But there is Robert Bakewell's famous iron 'Birdcage' (see Chapter 8) at Melbourne Hall in Derbyshire, obviously influenced by it, which can afford a splendid idea of how elaborate English work must have been. Wood treillage may be seen at Dropmore House, Buckinghamshire (plate 249), Shrubland Park in Suffolk, Belmont Park in Kent, Weston Park in Staffordshire (plate 250), and Bodnant Gardens, Denbighshire (plate 248).

Treillage has often been used to disguise uninteresting walls in town gardens, or to give, by false perspective, an impression of greater spaciousness. In they words of Shirley Hibberd (*Rustic Adornments*, 1857), 'trellis-work . . . certainl has a transforming power, as effectual as Harlequin's wand, and in a manner at once simple and inexpensive'. Such work may be seen in London in the gardens of the Savile Club, Brook Street, W.1, and Albany, Piccadilly. Many private houses in Chelsea and other London residential districts have examples.

False perspectives of treillage brings us to trompe l'œil—decoration designed to deceive the eye. The earliest such device must be the ha-ha, a hidden ditch with one vertical wall effectively excluding cattle from the garden, yet giving the impression of an uninterrupted landscape. There are ha-has in many parks and gardens.

Trompe l'œil has many forms—flat surfaces painted to look three-dimensional, mirrors arranged to give the impression of a gateway into another garden, foreshortening of the perspective of paths and vistas to make them look longer and, as we have just seen, treillage.

Such devices are not restricted to town gardens, though they there have obvious advantages. They are used effectively at Portmeirion, Merionethshire, where flat sheets of metal are effectively painted to look from a distance like true statues. In a garden at Montpelier Place in London a wall is painted as a three-dimensional architectural fantasia, complete with rustication and statuary. In a garden at Grosvenor Street, also in London, a mirror is arranged in an arbour to reflect an avenue of laurels, giving the impression that it is twice its actual length.

All of this may be reversed, and the garden apparently brought indoors. This effect was achieved by the murals painted by the late Rex Whistler in the dining-room of the Marquess of Anglesey at Plas Newydd on the Isle of Anglesey.

248 Trellis-work used imaginatively to form a pergola at Bodnant, Denbighshire.

249 Part of the 200-yard-long trellis pergola at Dropmore, Buckinghamshire. The whole structure is treated architecturally, with simulated arches, pilasters, pediments, cornices and friezes. It was probably constructed originally about the mid nineteenth century.

250 Trellis-work in a variety of patterns round the 'Swiss' cottage in the grounds of Weston Park, Staffordshire.

251 Treillage used with trompe l'œil effect in a London garden.

252 A trompe l'œil painting in the pavilion built in 1711 at Wrest Park, Bedfordshire, by Thomas Archer for Henry, Duke of Kent.

10 Paving

The most important path in the garden usually connects the house with the entrance, or with a garden focal point, or even, very naturally, with the compost heap. The material of the path, in order to be appropriate as well as serviceable, can vary greatly from dignity to rusticity while travelling from the entrance to the rubbish heap, and while the nether end can be of gravel or broken bricks, those portions around the house should set the standard for the rest of the garden—as indeed the house itself, preferably, should dominate and influence the design of its surrounds. For dignity, quality and the best walking surface, rectangular stone paving undoubtedly stands before all other materials. In front of a classic house it is ideal. As we progress away from the house the paving can become less uniform; garden design often becomes less formal away from the straight lines of the house. Other materials can be incorporated with the stone flags; perhaps ribbon-work such as was employed by Lutyens and Jekyll in many of their gardens, where lines of bricks, set herring-bone fashion, might be outlined by paving and perhaps with a selvedge of cobbles. Or the pattern, still less formal, might be conceived not longitudinally, but in repetitive style down the path. The transition from rectangular paving, through bricks used rectangularly or diagonally, then through old square street cobbles to seashore pebbles, takes us from the formal to the informal; and to vary these with old roofing-tiles laid flat or on edge, odd squares of stone, bottle bases, staddle-stone tops and millstones is like the transition from the formal classic house to the half-timbered cottage, or from the pillared gazebo to the potting-shed. There is a style of paving suitable for every kind of garden. Usually a path or a paved area is complementary but subsidiary to the general design, but in a featureless garden a path can well be of a dominant character, particularly if it has a fascinating pattern like the circle at the Old Dutch House at Sandwich in Kent (plate 262).

Crazy paving has its uses for informal paths and areas where no definite outline is desired; here the planting can take advantage of the broken edge of the paving. This style of paving may be said to come into its own in such areas, while if used for formal paths it savours of makeshift cheapness and suburban pettiness. Seldom used in this country, but found occasionally in the United States and elsewhere, are wood blocks and wood rounds (sections of trunks) used for paths, areas and steps where an informal and near-to-nature effect is required. Redwood is a popular, long-lasting timber where obtainable, but any timber that is used will have a comparatively short life.

For modern buildings of concrete and glass, concrete is to the fore today. The surfaces vary from the ordinary quality to various finishes; they may be tinted, or given an imitation roughness or a pattern; may be of fine sand finish or of deliberate pebble surface. The nearest in appearance to stone flags is reconstituted stone, which is often given an imitation sawn surface. To these newer materials brick and tile and cobble can well be added according to suitability, though they might be considered too rustic for the more modern schemes, except to achieve patterns. With rectangular concrete paving a large plaid pattern can be made by separating the squares with bricks on edge, or tiles.

Occasionally an elaborate design is desired, as for the floor of a small garden house, the centrepiece of a junction of paths, or as a permanent 'doormat' in front of the entrance to a dwelling. Small cobbles of different colours can be placed alongside tiles on edge; drainage pipes set to create a series of rings filled in with a mosaic of pebbles or coloured marbles; thin bricks, bottle bases and the like. Knuckle-bones of deer have been used as at Bicton and Killerton, both in Devon.

Any kind of paving is best made weed-proof and frost-resistant by setting in concrete. Paving, concrete, bricks and all large material can also be set in sand, but in time weeds will be a nuisance. For old roofing-tiles and thin materials a two-inch floor of concrete should be laid down, and when partially or fully set, the paving material, soaked in water, should be gently pressed into a covering of cement-mortar. Cobbles can be set in mud if large or if small in cement-mortar. It is best to use the cobbles with their smallest surface uppermost. Sand or sandy soil is best for laying wood blocks.

While many of the above materials are easily obtainable, some garden owners may prefer to make their own concrete slabs. Tinting powder can be obtained so that varied surface tones can be achieved. A set of, say, six rectangular wooden frames can be filled with the mixture, first scattering the frame-floors with the desired finishing material—sand, pebbles, chipped stone, etc. Alternatively, a set of frames of different sizes can be arranged so that the resulting slabs are of assorted but marriageable dimensions.

A great variety of paving styles and patterns in the traditions outlined above can be found at Hidcote, Gloucestershire; Sissinghurst, Kent; Tintinhull and Barrington Court, Somerset (plate 255); Portmeirion, Merionethshire (plates 263 and 265); Mount Vernon, Virginia, U.S.A.; Vasaparken, Stockholm, Sweden; the Shell building, London; Folly Farm, Berkshire.

253 Brick paving pattern at Bodnant, Denbighshire.

254 A variation of patterns in the walled garden at Trewithen, Cornwall. Sections of bricks laid in running bond alternate with sections laid in square formation.

255 Various patterns break up the monotony in this broad brick pathway at Barrington Court, Somerset.

256 Patterns in brick and knapped flints
in the courtyard of the Dower House,
Knowlton, Kent.

257 Brick and concrete paving patterns in
Mr Leonard Manasseh's London garden.
The concrete sculpture is by Daphne
Henrion-Hardy.

258 Paving pattern of concentric circles in the International Rosarium, s'Gravenhage, Netherlands.

259 A circular pathway in a rose garden in Kent. The tiles on edge solve the problem which arises when rectangular objects such as bricks are laid in a circle.

260 Curved brick pathway in modified basket-weave pattern in a garden in Kent.

261 Brick paths in simple running bond lead to the Lovers' Lane Pool at Dumbarton Oaks, Washington D.C., U.S.A.

262 Pebble mosaic and brick paving at The Old Dutch House, Sandwich, Kent.

263 Cobble stones, concrete stepping stones and kerbstones used effectively at Portmeirion, Merionethshire.

264 Rick stones or staddle stones, used as an edging to a pathway of random stone at Hodnet Hall, Shropshire.

265 Mosaic paving patterns at Portmeirion, Merionethshire.

266 Patterns in a paved area in a garden in Saffron Walden, Essex.

267 Pre-cast concrete slabs of different sizes and textures, used to form pathways.

267

268 Pre-cast concrete slabs surrounded by
cobbles form this path in a Hampshire
garden.

269 Lines of concrete slabs separated by flint cobbles.

270 Informal stone slabs form the pathway; the 'paved' area consists of granite chips set in cement in this nursery garden in the Netherlands.

271 A Monohex layout showing the use of hexagonal pre-cast concrete slabs of different textures, together with hexagonal tree grilles for root ventilation.

272 The main part of this paved area is made up of coarse exposed aggregate slabs.

273 The stepping stones up this rocky bank are made of disks of pre-cast exposed aggregate concrete.

274 Disks of pre-cast concrete in various sizes, the interstices filled with loose chippings.

275 Interlocking pre-cast concrete paving slabs in a nursery garden in the Netherlands.

276 Patterns in pebbles at Powerscourt, County Wicklow, Eire.

277 Pre-cast concrete slabs in various colours and textures are used to form a pathway in this garden in Fulda, West Germany, designed by Professor Hermann Mattern.

278 Paved fountain in a garden in Oerlinghausen, West Germany, designed by Professor Hermann Mattern.

279 Paving in a garden at Glumslöv, Sweden, designed by Professor Mattern.

280 Paving of a Roman bath at Schloss Charlottenburg, Sans-Souci, Potsdam, East Germany.

281 Patterns in cobbles at the Villa
Gamberaia, Florence, Italy.

282 Stepping stones in a garden in Kyoto,
Honshu, Japan.

11 Garden Furniture

The furnishing of gardens with objects of utility and beauty is a subject of immense scope, since it might legitimately be considered that plants, pools, lawns and lakes are the furnishings of a site. Taking a leaf from a valuer's notebook, however, it might be more sensible to separate furniture from fitments and to define furniture in gardens as movable objects of decoration and use such as statuary, seats, tables, plant-tubs and pots.

If this is our definition, it can be stated that few garden owners used garden furniture until the nineteenth century. In the monumental tradition of Italy, France and Britain up to the seventeenth century, garden seats and alcoves were usually of marble and stone and were used rather as terminal features for vistas than as places for rest and relaxation.

In the ornamented farms and early landscape gardens of the eighteenth century, garden seats were considered to be suitable punctuation marks in a pictorial composition and were placed at view points. The seats at the Leasowes in Shropshire, by William Shenstone, were, for example, inscribed with a few appropriate lines from Virgil or Horace to give the visitor a clue as to the associations and trains of thought which the view could be expected to stimulate. In all these instances garden seats were used as fixed elements in the design.

By the nineteenth century the landscape garden had become the domestic villa garden, and it was thought that the same principles should be observed in designing it as in furnishing a room. Hence the fashion for carpet-bedding which attempted to furnish the 'exquisite verdure' of a lawn with flowers arranged in imitation of the patterns of an Axminster carpet. Seats and ornamental urns were an obvious addition to the *décor* of an open-air drawing-room with its outdoor carpet, seats, sofas and flower-baskets. During the cult of rusticity popular in this period cast-iron seats made to look like rustic logs, seats using fern leaves as motifs (see plates 293 and 294) and seats of elegant wire-work and varnished wood provided the necessary but not very comfortable resting-places.

The 'umbrella' was a not unusual feature of this period. Many of these were in the form of thatched shelters for the circular seats at their base, or were timbered and tiled.

Garden furniture of the present day is associated with the uses to which we now put our gardens, which are designed not principally for the purpose of composing a picture, stimulating a mood or for horticultural education, but by and large to create an islanded hour or so of peace and relaxation. Hence the upholstery which has been introduced into modern garden furniture, now designed for casual cushioned comfort.

The deck-chair, the most popular unit of garden furniture ever to be manufactured, and now international in its uses, is one of the ingenious inventions for which we have to thank the Merchant Navy in the hey-day of our Empire at the end of the nineteenth century. Its blessings are many. Not only is it used to provide comedians with endless opportunities for clowning, but it is light, cheap and comfortable.

It is the belief in the therapeutic value of the sun—resulting in the cult of sunbathing—that has stimulated the design and manufacture of casual, weatherproof, comfortable and colourful furniture in those countries where the sun is most generously visible. And so it is that the Americans and Italians, the French and the Scandinavians, lead in the design of nylon-coated steel chairs, chaise-longues and tables, of barbecues and their fitments, of awnings, sun-umbrellas and hammocks.

Architects of the immediate post-war generation also concerned themselves with the design of plant containers for use in gardens and public open spaces, town concourses and piazzas. Earthenware plant pots have been redesigned and revived for use in small town gardens. Assembled groups of these, planted with annuals and perennials, have proved a decorative and eminently manageable addition to the small town garden.

283 Eighteenth-century stone seat with finely carved ends, at Stourhead, Wiltshire.

284 Finely carved eighteenth-century marble seat, with winged lion ends, at Stanton Harcourt Manor, Oxfordshire.

285 An Italian stone semicircular seat, supported by winged lions, the panels carved with vine motifs, the finials carved to represent the cones of the stone-pine.

286 An elaborately carved seat in the Italian garden at Westonbirt School, Gloucestershire.

287 Portland stone seat with carved ends representing a swan and boy, at Knightshayes Court, Devon.

288 Simple seat, made from an old stone sink, at East Lambrook Manor, Somerset.

289 'Gothic' garden seat (once much longer but now reduced in length) at Barrow Court, Somerset.

290 Regency cast-iron and wirework garden day-bed, *c.* 1810.

291 Victorian iron garden seat in a Gloucestershire garden.

292 Iron garden seat, possibly part of a set designed to surround a tree trunk, and probably Victorian in origin, photographed in a Gloucestershire garden.

293 Cast-iron seats with fern-leaf motif, at Portmeirion, Merionethshire.

294 'Fern-leaf' pattern seat in the gardens of The Owl House, Lamberhurst, Kent.

295 Wooden seat in the Abbey Garden, Bury St Edmunds, Suffolk.

296 'Wheelbarrow' seat at Trewithen, Cornwall. Seats of this kind may be traced back to the eighteenth century; another pattern was designed by Sir Edwin Lutyens.

297 Lightweight metal seats based on a 'Strawberry Hill' Gothic design, made for Sunningdale Nurseries, Surrey, a few years ago.

298 Seat at Portmeirion, Merionethshire.

299 Lightweight metal seats in the garden behind the Museum van het Boek, The Hague, Netherlands, originally in the garden of one of the Royal Dutch Palaces.

300 Nineteenth-century cast-iron bench with wooden seat at Borgestad, near Porsgrunn, Norway.

301 Stone table and stools in the small garden of the Forbidden City, Peking, China.

302 Octagonal seat with canopy in the gardens of Schloss Nymphenburg, Munich, West Germany.

12 Topiary

Topiary is a peculiar fashion of gardening that has existed since Roman days or earlier, consisting of clipping bushes into geometric or fancy shapes. (*Topiarius* is Latin for ornamental gardening or one who works at it.) The tradition has arrived in modern gardens through the influence of great Italian and French gardens and had a great vogue in Holland in the seventeenth century; a further vogue came about during the second half of the nineteenth century in Britain, when labour was still cheap and many big gardens were still being made. Topiary ranges from the great clipped avenues at Versailles down to the smallest box edging, and from huge peacocks perched on top of living obelisks to the tiny 'teddy bear' clipped to fancy in a cottage garden. At Versailles, at Howth Castle, Dublin, and at Meiklour, Perthshire, Scotland, clipping of deciduous native trees (beech or lime) may ascend to twenty-five feet or more. Quickthorn was used long ago but today is seldom seen clipped except along the roadside, a quirk or enthusiasm of some earnest labourer. Yew is undoubtedly the most excellent evergreen for the work as it is sturdy and dense, but the fragrant box is also very popular; it unfortunately gets loose with age. *Lonicera nitida*, privets, holly and many other dense shrubs can be used; and for quick effect *Cupressocyparis leylandii*. Although many old specimens have developed in the slow way of moulding the bush by clipping, a much speedier method is to manure heavily a young bush, encouraging it to make vigorous growth in all directions, and then to train its branches onto wire frames. Given the initial growth and the frame, a 'peacock' can be made complete in a space of, say, four years.

Apart from isolated specimens in various gardens, whole areas within gardens have been devoted to topiary, witness the great yew collections at Levens Hall, Westmorland (plate 307), and Compton Wynyates, Warwickshire (plate 305); the noted 'chessmen' at Haseley Court, Oxfordshire (plate 306), and Chilham Castle, Kent (plate 315); animal shapes at Melksham Court, Gloucestershire; golden yew parasols at Chatsworth in Derbyshire and Hever Castle in Kent. In Ireland two examples are the ornamented lawn at Headfort, Co. Meath, and the beds on the terraces at Powerscourt where box edgings contain raised platforms of yew. Packwood in Warwickshire (plate 304) has some of the tallest and oldest clipped yews in the country; these are all formal or regular shapes, representing in their multitude the Sermon on the Mount. Also we find the entirely informal shapes where bushes of yew have been clipped over for many years by devoted craftsmen, such as the numerous isolated examples in churchyards and village gardens, and the cumulus-like series of arches at Headfort.

In ruder times the clipping of bushes and the ordering of vistas and the like may be taken as an expression of man's relief at having control over his landscape and plants; time was taken for gardening, safely enclosed, away from the dangers of the countryside, and man's will was imposed upon nature. Later it became a fashion or a conceit. Thereafter, while the trend of gardening became ever more complex, deriving its inspiration from earlier gardens in every country, we may consider topiary as an embellishment, used often to excess, in gardens of the last hundred years or so. As an art it seems to fit the two extremes of gardening best; we may enjoy both the careful pride of the cottager who devotes years to training a fantastic shape of greenery by his front gate, and the extensive range of shapes seen in our greater gardens. But the average garden of one or two acres of today is seldom the place to indulge in whimsy; here surely the formal hedge and occasional geometrical design may be enjoyed alone. In this category we can place the topiary at Hidcote, Gloucestershire (plate 309), and Tintinhull, Somerset, where it becomes part of the design. At Montacute, Somerset, and Shugborough and Lyme Park, both in Staffordshire, the conical clipped yews become the dominant theme recurring through the garden. At Powis Castle, Montgomeryshire (plate 5), the thirty-foot yews appear to buttress the very walls of the castle. At Nymans, Sussex, the sculptured effect dominates an otherwise informally planted walled garden. Other good English examples are at Kingston Russell House, Dorset; Ludstone Hall, Shropshire; Sandringham, Norfolk; Sedgwick Park, Sussex; St Nicholas, Yorkshire (plate 316); Mapperton, Dorset (plate 317); Blickling Hall, Norfolk; Ascott, Buckinghamshire (plate 310); and Knightshayes Court, Devon (plate 311).

303 Yew arbour, about thirty feet high and 200 years old, at Antony House, Cornwall. Clipped once a year, using a fire-escape ladder, it is a fine and unusual example of topiary.

304 In the Yew Garden at Packwood House, Warwickshire. The yews, planted in the late seventeenth century, are said to represent the Sermon on the Mount: twelve larger specimens representing the apostles, four even larger at the centre representing the evangelists. Heights range from twenty-five feet or so upwards.

305 Topiary at Compton Wynyates,
Warwickshire, near the house which was
rebuilt in Tudor times.

306 In the 'Chessboard' garden at Haseley Court, Oxfordshire. The topiary specimens were probably planted in the 1860s.

307 Part of the well-known topiary garden at Levens Hall, Westmorland. The specimens in box and yew are trimmed into various curious shapes, including the great umbrella seen on the right.

308 A massive topiary gateway of simple design at Rous Lench Court, Worcestershire.

309 A neatly clipped topiary arch and various bird shapes at Hidcote Manor, Gloucestershire.

310 Topiary sundial at Ascott, Buckinghamshire, in which various evergreens, including variegated and other coloured forms, are used for the gnomon and the hour numerals.

311 Running hounds endlessly pursue a fox at Knightshayes Court, Devon.

312 Topiary in a cottage garden at Sapperton, Gloucestershire.

313 In the Japanese Gardens, Tully, County Kildare, Eire, designed about 1906.

314 Early twentieth-century topiary in the garden designed by Gertrude Jekyll at The Salutation, Sandwich, Kent.

315 Some of the yews, clipped to represent chessmen, on the lower terrace at Chilham Castle, Kent.

316 Closely clipped yew hedges at St Nicholas, Richmond, Yorkshire, planted in 1906.

317 In the terraced garden at Mapperton, Dorset.

318 Carefully clipped yew hedges, planted since 1930, form the 'Rondel' at Sissinghurst Castle, Kent.

319 Carefully clipped hedges and topiary specimens in the Papal Garden at Castelgandolfo, Italy.

320 The reconstructed garden of the Governor's Palace, Colonial Williamsburg, Virginia, U.S.A.

321 The Rose Garden and Topiary
Garden at Longwood, Pennsylvania,
U.S.A.

322 Formal shapes in the gardens of the
Governor's Palace, Colonial Williamsburg.

13 Knots and Parterres

The laying out of intricate geometrical patterns, marked out with plants, or with plants and a mixture of coloured earths or minerals, is a practice of considerable antiquity in the history of gardening.

It must surely have as its origin an adaptation of the mosaic to garden design. In its simpler forms such a pattern is called a knot-garden. (The word used in this connection, though rather vaguely, first appears in the English language at the end of the fourteenth century.)

The earliest published designs for knots resemble strap-work patterns—the ornamentation of flat surfaces that is found, for example, in Dutch architecture. Sometimes they were connected with heraldry. The outline was usually traced in living green; closely trimmed box was the most usual material, but other low-growing plants such as rosemary and thrift were also used. A knot-garden consisted of several rectangles set closely together, each one probably containing a different pattern. One could walk between them.

By the middle of the seventeenth century we find that the word knot is replaced by parterre: France had now superseded Italy as the inspiration of garden design. The simpler patterns have become elaborated and enlarged; one flowing design covers the whole area of a parterre.

By the early eighteenth century, when the French parterre was at its best, the patterns were taken from geometrical figures, 'branched and flourished work', palms, foliage, 'hawk's-bills', sprigs, tendrils, frets, interlacings, wreaths, 'shell-works of grass' and other motifs.

The finest and most magnificent of all were the *parterres de broderie*, formed of box to imitate the free design of embroidery set out upon the earth. The major part of the background was sanded, the finer details being filled in with 'smith's dust' or black earth.

Parterres de compartiment consisted, as the name implies, of a number of compartments of 'scrolls, grass works, knots and borders of flowers' symmetrically arranged. The ground of these was again sand, the paths between being of powdered tile-shards or brick-dust.

Parterres à l'anglaise, introduced from England, were 'the plainest and meanest of all', being grass plots 'but little cut into shapes'.

Cut-work parterres consisted of a number of shaped beds, cut symmetrically, lined with box edging and filled with flowers. These were surrounded with sanded paths upon which one could walk; other materials used were spar, pit-coal and gravel.

The parterres were placed next to the house, of such a size and proportion that the eye, when near the building (which was raised above the surrounding garden), could take in and comprehend the pattern at one glance.

The gardener was warned that, unlike other parts of a garden, a parterre was at its best when it was first planted, the box in due course spreading, the earth losing its level and the grass sometimes not 'preserving its primitive beauty. . . .' 'But these, indeed,' we read, 'are things inevitable, notwithstanding all the cost and pains we can bestow.'

The final stage of the parterre was the introduction during the nineteenth century of the brilliantly coloured half-hardy plants and annuals set out in late spring, when the risk of frost was over, in designs which ranged from those in the French tradition to floral representations of such scenes as the 'Teddy Bears' Picnic'.

323 The garden at Moseley Old Hall, Staffordshire, laid out in recent years by the National Trust in the style of Charles II, showing the box parterre with tinted gravels and, to the left, the wooden alley.

324 The parterre garden at Oxburgh Hall, Norfolk, laid out about 1845, copied from an unknown French garden.

325 Looking down from the terrace at Cliveden, Buckinghamshire, on to the bold parterre designs in the great lawn.

326 Parterres in the Fountain Garden at Lyme Park, Cheshire.

327 The Italianate parterres at Drummond Castle, Perthshire, as seen from the terraces.

328 The knot garden and garden house at Pollok House, Glasgow.

329 The reconstructed seventeenth-century 'great garden' at Pitmedden, Aberdeenshire. There are four large parterres which include in their design the Saltire and Thistle and the arms of Sir Alexander Seton (late seventeenth century) as well as patterns used in the layout of the garden at Holyrood House, Edinburgh.

330 The intricate, box-edged parterre in the restored Renaissance gardens of the Château de Villandry, Indre-et-Loire, France.

331 At the Château de Chenonceaux, Indre-et-Loire, another French Renaissance garden, the parterre and the topiary are simpler in form.

332 A parterre at the Schloss Schleissheim, near Munich, West Germany.

333 Looking down on the vast parterre at Versailles, Seine-et-Oise, France.

334 In the gardens of the Palace of Queluz, Lisbon, Portugal's 'little Versailles'.

335 The lower parterre garden at the Villa Lante, Bagnaia, Italy, with its central fountain and plant containers of various kinds. The layout has changed very little since the mid seventeenth century.

14 Rustic Adornments

Why and when did the word 'rustic', of so wide and generally accepted a meaning as 'to do with the country', acquire the specialized meaning now found in dictionaries of 'made of untrimmed branches'? This usage seems to derive from the construction of buildings in the escapist, rural style that was characteristic of the late eighteenth-century picturesque manner. J. C. Loudon wrote in 1827:

Roofed seats, boat-houses, moss houses, flint houses, bark huts and similar constructions, are different modes of forming resting places . . . very neat buildings and furniture of this class may be formed of hazel-rods, or any tree with a clean bark and straight shoots, as young oaks or mountain ash. The spruce fir affords a good material, and five or six young trees coupled together make good rustic columns.

He also refers to 'gates in garden scenery, when architectural elegance is not required to support character, simple or rustic structures . . . may be introduced according to the character of the scene'.

A few decades later, in Shirley Hibberd's popular *Rustic Adornments for Homes of Taste*, among his many other 'rustic adornments' we get details of rustic summer-houses of which 'the coat or shell must be of rough branches', of rustic pot stands, and of pergolas made of rough branches—which were no more than the usual forms of garden decoration then fashionable in middle class suburban gardens, but reflecting a townsman's idea of the country. Nor does the architect's specialized term 'rustication' help us.

It seems probable that the great popular era of 'rustic work' and the widespread use of the term came about with the general availability of very large numbers of larch poles at the end of the last century. They were of little use for any other purpose, and the 'rustic adornment' market is still the most profitable one for the forester's larch-thinnings.

The great era of wooden rustic adornments was the first half of the nineteenth century. Though known in the eighteenth century, their vogue does not seem to have flourished much earlier: the rural qualities of Marie Antoinette's Trianon seem to have been achieved in much more substantial materials.

The zenith of this transient form of architecture was surely reached in the moss house. This was the Victorian equivalent of the Georgian grotto with its interior shell-work or collection of crystals. Instead the moss was an exterior embellishment providing, incidentally, a lesson in living cryptogams. A wooden garden house was built, with a portico supported by uprights made from tree trunks, and with curved cross-pieces forming Gothic arches. Within this framework the walls of the building were formed in square panels on which were nailed—in such shapes as stars, lozenges, and triangles—rods of wood, close together. In between these rods mosses were carefully wedged— having been carefully chosen for colour and texture (and correctly named botanically)—so that, when established, they hid the rods that held them. These gave an evenness of surface, closeness of texture and variety of colour not unlike those of a Turkey carpet. Added refinements were windows of stained glass and a cornice of pine-cones.

As a contrast, there was the more typical building described in Dickens's *Pickwick Papers*; the sweet retreat for spiders, over which straggled honeysuckle and jessamine, and within which happened the famous episode involving Mr Tracy Tupman and Miss Wardle.

And this shows us the weakness of rustic work. The knobbly, angular, bark-covered branches which were essential to the aesthetics of its construction provided good harbourage not only for spiders but for the spores of every rotting fungus, as well as wood-lice and the other unromantic wild life associated with rusticity.

No doubt this was the reason why cast-iron was called in to bring permanence to that particular piece of woodwork in which strength was essential: the rustic bench. The legs and framework were cast in the image of tortuous branches. The advance of science made it possible for these to achieve a combination of delicacy, slenderness and strength that could not be matched by the clumsier, frailer oak branches. The actual seat and back were of carefully planed oak, attached to the iron rusticity with nuts and bolts. A more surprising substitute for wood was terra-cotta and similar heavy pottery, brightly coloured.

Perhaps this justifies the somewhat restrained enthusiasm that we find in G. W. Johnson's *Gardener's Dictionary* of 1856:

Rustic structures are pleasing structures in recluse portions of the pleasure-ground, if this style be confined to the formation of either a seat or a cottage; but it is ridiculous if complicated and elegant forms are constructed of rude materials. Thus we have seen a flower-box, intended to be Etruscan in its outlines, formed of split hazel stakes—a combination of the rude and refined, giving rise to separate trains of ideas totally unassociable.

With the present vogue for Victoriana, we may well look forward to the 'totally unassociable' idea of rustic work in aluminium and, no doubt, plastic.

336 Rustic seat at Northbourne Court, Kent.

337 Thatched rustic summer-house at Henley Hall, Shropshire.

338 Rustic bridges in the gardens of The Owl House, Lamberhurst, Kent.

339 A larger but still essentially simple wooden bridge at Leonardslee, Sussex.

340 Rustic wooden bridge in a bungalow garden in Lahore, West Pakistan.

341 Simple rustic bridge in a Devonshire cottage garden

PART II
Garden Buildings

Introduction

The garden was originally a part of, or at least an extension to, the house. It might be no more than a courtyard furnished with a splashing fountain and some herbage virtually within the house, as is seen today in Moorish architecture. Or, as we observe it in numerous medieval Books of Hours, a small, enclosed, cosy place, again with fountains, a few trees and railed flower beds close to the house. The monastery garden, primarily for the purpose of growing medicinal herbs, yet of great importance in the history of botany and horticulture, was but a small area within the precincts of the complex of monastic buildings. The Italian Renaissance garden, developed from its Roman predecessors, was, as Edith Wharton pointed out, adapted to the architectural lines of the villa, providing an accessible extension to it wherein the pleasures of the fresh air were to hand and from which the beauty of the surrounding landscape could be enjoyed.

As late as the seventeenth century it was still assumed that the garden would be a walled enclosure intimately connected with the house. Man is unlike his enemy the snail in at least one particular: he does not carry his house with him. And when he wanders abroad, even in so restricted a space as his garden (and gardens became more spacious in Renaissance times), he seems to have an urge to cover and roof himself in. In the Mediterranean lands it is to protect him from the sun; in northern lands, from the treacherous showers and the deadly north and east winds. Also, wherever he may be, he seems to have a prejudice against alfresco meals and prefers to eat within a building.

Apart from this, as a horticulturist he discovered at an early stage that a number of plants—possibly the fruiting trees that a millennium or more ago found their way to Europe from the remote mountains of western and central China, and which were the reason for his original experiments—could, like him, prosper only if they had a roof over their heads.

Around these requirements man has produced much delightful and some significant architecture.

It is surprising that, although the garden was closely connected with the house for so long, the fact that its walls provided warm situations on which to grow tender plants and ripen choice fruit was a comparatively late discovery. The Romans, we know, liked to train ivy and other evergreens against their buildings to give greenery in winter and freshness in the heat of summer, yet they seem not to have progressed beyond this. The practice of growing fruit on walls in the British Isles was not remarked upon until early in the seventeenth century, after which it was (like all matters horticultural) rapidly developed.

The practice of growing and ripening the fruit of tender plants within, as opposed to against, walls is, however, of some antiquity. Pliny the Elder and Columella, both writing in the first century A.D., refer to it. The windows of the buildings were covered with sheets of talc. Martial on one occasion rather acidly pointed out that his host's fruit trees were so protected, whereas his bedroom windows remained uncovered.

It is amusing to speculate on which of the two apparently earliest forms of garden structure came first—the trellis or the garden house. Both existed in Egyptian gardens of 1000 B.C.

In China, where the house and garden were from early times one integrated unit of an entirely different type from that in the West, the garden house was an important feature of the T'ang Dynasty gardens—that is from the seventh century A.D.

In the West, the whole range of garden pleasure buildings were already found in Rome. They were described, with all their enjoyments—physical, mental and visual—by the younger Pliny as they existed in his garden of the first century A.D. At the end of a topiary walk

is an alcove of white marble, shaded by vines, supported by four Carystian pillars. From a bench, the water gushing through several little pipes, as if it were pressed out by the weight of the persons who repose upon it, falls into a stone cistern underneath, from whence it is received into a fine polished marble basin, so artfully contrived that it is always full without ever overflowing. . . . When I sup here, this basin serves for a table, the larger sort of dishes being placed round the margin, while the smaller ones swim about in the form of little vessels and water-fowl. Fronting the alcove . . . stands a summer-house of exquisite marble, the doors whereof project and open into a green enclosure; from its upper and lower windows the eye is presented with a variety of verdures. Next to this is a little private recess (which, though it seems distinct may be laid into the same room) furnished with a couch; and notwithstanding it has windows on every side, yet it enjoys a very agreeable gloominess, by means of a spreading vine which climbs to the top and entirely overshades it. Here you may recline and fancy yourself in a wood; with this difference only—that you are not exposed to the weather. In this place a fountain also rises and instantly disappears; in different quarters are disposed marble seats which serve, no less than the summer-house, as so many reliefs after one is wearied with walking.

Here were all the elements—indeed, an array of them—that were long forgotten and became once again the features of the Italian garden several centuries later. These classical models were to set the pattern of most garden buildings until the nineteenth century. (One feels that the Romans would have delighted in modern plastic ducks to float and take part in their fountain-table meals.)

The gardens of Rome were inspired by the ideals of perfection in architectural design—and luxury. Equally architectural in execution, with exquisite buildings, were the gardens of East and Near East, but yet with an entirely different inspiration—that of symbolism, indeed mysticism. This type of garden originated in India, moved to China and thence to Japan, by which time the buildings had become incidentals rather than the core of the design.

One day, perhaps, some scholar will work out the migration, as it were, of gardening ideas and designs from the Orient to the West, which no doubt filtered into the Roman gardens via Greece and certainly, at a much later date, arrived in Spain from North Africa. This influence, however, is remote, and the architecture and garden buildings of Europe, and those continents such as North America whose aesthetics were based on the European patterns, are surely primarily materialistic and neither mystical nor symbolical.

Next to the array of garden houses, the major structural buildings in gardens are terraces and walls. The former no doubt developed from the crude forms essential to agriculture in hilly land, and, by the Italians in particular, were raised to works of consummate architecture. Walls belong more to flatter terrain, having their obvious origin in the need to keep undesirable mammals (particularly man) out, but being eventually developed as decorative structures and aids to horticulture.

The terraced garden in suitable surroundings can be the supreme expression of garden art. It is a profoundly unnatural structure in which every artifice can be employed. Stairways may have their flights set at an angle one to another, or may sweep up and down in curves, their balustradings richly ornamented. The levelled platforms can be wide and calm, or narrow, hanging high and excitingly above the landscape. Summer-houses may terminate these walks; fountains, fed by water from the high ground above, interrupt them. For those interested in horticulture, every aspect is available for planting—as long as architectural detail is not obscured. (An admirable example is seen in one of the few eighteenth-century terrace gardens in the British Isles, at Powis Castle in Montgomeryshire. It was possibly designed at the end of the seventeenth century by Captain William Winde, an expert in fortifications.)

The use of walls to enclose gardens was universal until they were 'thrown down' by the landscapers in the eighteenth century. When times ceased to be troubled and walls were not essential, they were still frequently used, designed to be a feature of the garden. The necessary massive base, usually of stone (until concrete arrived in the nineteenth century), could be a handsome feature. The coping was carried out in a variety of manners. The buttresses too (also often coped) played their part in a design that, though functional, was devised to give pleasure. Particularly in the French gardens, *claires-voies*—framed openings for observation of the view through decorative wrought-ironwork or railings—were effectively used. The Dutch, on the other hand, developed the wall for purely horticultural purposes.

Of other garden buildings, the orangery was for several centuries primarily a *tour de force* of minor architecture involving the decorative treatment of large areas of glass. This was probably the result of its popularization in the France of Le Nôtre. Not until the late eighteenth or even early nineteenth century was it treated as a building primarily constructed for horticultural purposes, by which time it had deteriorated architecturally into the conservatory. With the development in England of the landscape garden (begun in the early eighteenth century), with its spread to Europe and far beyond as *le jardin anglais*, and with its subsequent transition to the romantically picturesque, the architect stepped down from his powerful, over-riding position as garden designer. He became only the creator of the very numerous minor buildings that were now no more than 'eye-catchers' or incidents in the scene. From what had been a whole range of temples and analogous buildings 'in variety' of fine architectural quality, garden buildings had, by the end of that century, evolved into such oddities as a 'substantially built' ruin of a Roman aqueduct, 'very well managed' ruins of the Temple of Mercury, and a 'very magnificent' Turkish mosque.

Today the terraced garden in the grand manner has long been a thing of the past; in England it passed away with a singularly glorious last gasp in Barry's great design at Shrubland Park in Suffolk, carried out in the middle of the last century. Garden houses, summer-houses and loggias—even temples—of admirable design continued to be built into the early decades of the present century, then to be replaced by mass-produced, very practical wooden structures, '. . . easily erected without skilled labour'.

One form of structure with a long lineage, usually constructed now under the aegis of a municipal authority, continues to be 'architect designed'—sometimes with imagination. The Italian Renaissance banqueting-house, a substantial and highly ornamental building, standing on its own in the garden, arrived as far north as England at the time when Henry VIII was building his then very modern palace of Nonsuch. Its purpose was not the provision of those substantial, formal meals we now class as banquets, but of sweets and light refreshments, combined sometimes with entertainment. Can we not regard the ingenious geometrically designed refreshment building near the Serpentine bridge in London, and a number of comparable buildings scattered over the world, as belonging to, and long survivors of, this centuries-old tradition—and as reminders that gardeners once employed supreme architects to embellish their gardens?

15 Gatehouses

There are two main kinds of gatehouse: large structures, often wholly or partly fortified, originating in the Middle Ages, but which continued to be built until the nineteenth century; and smaller buildings, often pretty and ornate, usually lodges for gatekeepers.

An early English example of the former kind, not originally part of a garden, is the embattled yet beautifully decorated abbey gateway at Bury St Edmunds (c. 1330–53), now the main entrance to the town's public gardens. Somewhat later (fifteenth-century), and in some ways even more impressive, is the gatehouse to the gardens of St Osyth's Priory, Essex, of flint panelwork, arranged with stone into Gothic and chequer patterns. Another, of similar date and equally elaborate, is at St John's Abbey, Colchester. Yet more examples, though of stone, are at Battle Abbey and Bodiam Castle, Sussex (both fourteenth-century), and Oxborough Hall, Norfolk (fifteenth-century). More recent is the stone and flint gatehouse at Eastwell Park, Kent (nineteenth-century) (plate 345).

A magnificent example of the sixteenth century is the gatehouse at Hardwick Hall in Derbyshire, with its cresting of stone coronet, strap-work and pyramids. It differs from the examples just mentioned in that it is purely a gatehouse, without living accommodation.

Some of the most pleasing of English brick-built gatehouses are at Cambridge; of these the best are at Trinity, St John's (both sixteenth-century) and Queens' Colleges (fifteenth-century), each leading from a busy street into a cool courtyard with lawns and flowers in beds or window-boxes. They are decorated with statuary and armorial devices which, emblazoned in their true tinctures, strike a pleasing note against the brickwork. But of all Cambridge college gatehouses, the prettiest is the Gate of Honour (completed 1575) at Gonville and Caius, now, alas, somewhat overpowered by its recently added sundials.

Oxford, too, has some fine stone gatehouses, especially those at Christ Church (Wolsey's gateway, sixteenth-century; Tom Tower added by Wren, 1682) and the Cattle Street entrance to All Souls' (Hawksmoor, 1720–56).

Other English gatehouses include those at West Drayton, Middlesex; Melford Hall, Suffolk; Westwood Park, Droitwich (sixteenth-century); the splendid specimen at the Oxford Physick Garden (c. 1645) with its statue of

Charles I; the two-storeyed gatehouse at Lanhydrock, Cornwall (seventeenth-century) (plate 343); the Coade stone classical gateway, lodges and screen at Easton Neston, Northamptonshire (William Croggan, 1822); and Sir John Soane's massive composition at Tyringham, Buckinghamshire (1795).

Excellent large gatehouses are in some of the London parks. An example is Hanover Gate, Regent's Park.

Outstanding among overseas gatehouses are the Arc de Triomphe du Carrousel (begun 1806, a reduced copy of the Arch of Septimius Severus, Rome) in the Tuileries Gardens, Paris; the Porte Dauphine, Fontainebleau (sixteenth-century); the Porte du Béguinage, Bruges (1776); the colourful tiled and polished marble portal of the Madrasa Mader-i-Shah of the Chahar Bagh (= Four Gardens) at Isfahan (1714); the classical gatehouse to Trinity College, Dublin (Keene and Sanderson, 1755–9); the baroque structure at the water garden of the Villa Foscari, Malcontenta (Andrea Palladio, *c.* 1560); and that at Vignola's water garden at Villa Lante, Bagnaia.

Of the second type of gatehouse, earlier English specimens were sometimes half-timbered, like the detached building at Stokesay Castle in Shropshire (sixteenth- and seventeenth-century). Some are reminiscent of Rockingham porcelain cottages. Such is the little round lodge (nineteenth-century) at Gog Magog House, Cambridgeshire, which has now, however, lost much of its charm from being enlarged, though the simple Gothic glazing of the windows remains. Near by, at Babraham, are others of similar date, with wood columns along their front elevation. Other romantic revival gatehouses are at Bulstrode (Gothic Revival, John Wyatt); Aston Hall, Warwickshire (Gothic Revival); the thatched Round Lodge, Bedfordshire; Daw's and Bridge Lodges at Moccas, Herefordshire (*c.* 1805); and the mock-castle gatehouse at Limerick Lodge, Lough Cutra, Co. Galway (*c.* 1815), all three by John Nash.

Poxwell Manor in Dorset has an earlier example in which a gateway is combined with a garden house, reached by an exterior stairway. It is built of brick, tile and stone and constructed so as to form part of a massive brick wall.

There is a fine baroque example at the seventeenth-century Antwerp house of Rubens; it is part of the house itself. The arch stretches across the courtyard, framing a view of the gardens, and is surmounted by balustrading, vases and statuary.

One of the most pleasing of modern gatehouses is at Sir Clough Williams-Ellis's super-folly, Portmeirion, Merionethshire, Wales. Painted peach and white, it is surmounted by elegant stone vases and reminds one of Wedgwood's jasper ware.

342 A rare fifteenth-century half-timbered gatehouse at Lower Brockhampton, Herefordshire.

343 Castellated gatehouse at Lanhydrock, Cornwall. The ball-topped pinnacle motif is repeated along the low castellated garden walls.

345 The mid nineteenth-century gatehouse at Eastwell Park, Kent, home of Alfred, Duke of Edinburgh, second son of Queen Victoria, and birthplace of Queen Marie of Rumania.

346 A mixture of styles can be seen in the gatehouse of Stanway House, Gloucestershire, built between 1640 and 1650. The Dutch gables are topped by scallop shells, a motif repeated elsewhere; the windows are Jacobean and Doric columns flank the archway.

344 The fifteenth-century gatehouse at Cerne Abbey, Dorset, now partially covered with climbing garden plants.

347 The gatehouse, Penrhyn Castle, Caernarvonshire, built between 1827 and 1846. It is an example of the Norman Revival style, a short-lived offshoot from the Gothic Revival.

348 The gatehouse at Ripley Castle, Yorkshire, dates back to 1418. On the left-hand tower is a clock, on the right a wind indicator.

16 Garden Houses

Secluded from this world, oh, let me dwell
With contemplation in this lonely cell;
By mortal eye unseen, I will explore
The various works of nature's bounteous store;
Revisit of each flower, whose blossom fair
With fragrant sweets perfumes the ambient air;
Pry into every shrub, and mark its way
From birth to death, from growth to sure decay. . . .

These highly moral lines come from Joseph Addison's 'Inscription in A Summer House'—a summer-house presumably erected in his garden at Bilton, near Rugby. Its significance is that Addison was a pioneer of the landscape garden—and that under this style of gardening, the only feature of the classical garden that survived (indeed proliferated) was the summer-house, or, as it was inappropriately called when first introduced to England from Italy via France, the shade house.

The garden house—that is, a place of refuge within the garden, remote from and unconnected with the mansion—seems to have originated in the *herbier*, in English 'arbour' or merely 'bower', a seat shaded by trees, shrubs or plants such as climbers, often clipped into a room-like shape.

There are the lines in the medieval poem, *The Flower and the Leaf*, referring to

. . . a pleasaunt herber well y wrought
That benched was and with turfes new . . .

And shapen was this herber roofe and all
As a pretty parlour: and also
The hegge as thicke as a castle wall . . .

A later line, 'he should not see if there were any wight within or no', foreshadows the opening words of Addison's poem.

In Italy a variation earlier than 1305 (when Pietro de Crescenzi published a description) was the arbour built up in a tree. At a suitable distance from the ground the branches were trained outwards, and a platform erected upon and within them. They were then trained to grow erect—so forming the walls—and, having reached sufficient height, were gathered in to make a roof. Above that, they were permitted to proceed as they wished, unhampered. Travellers on the Continent in succeeding centuries describe such tree-houses: Montaigne gives a detailed description of one at Schaffhausen in 1580 and Celia Fiennes of something similar at Woburn in 1697. A 'tree-house' of some age still exists at Pitchford in Shropshire (plate 368).

In China, garden tea-houses and more elaborate garden pavilions (plate 380) have a long history. Their design was not to affect the West until the eighteenth century, and then as a pastiche.

The summer-houses of the Italian Renaissance, as indeed in oriental or any other early gardens, were carried out in the normal architectural style of the period.

There are certain other buildings which may be classed as summer-houses. The Spanish glorieta, of Moorish origin, is one. It is defined as a special kind of arbour, 'a tiny paradise', a private glory. It is circular, in the belief that paradise is here equivalent to heaven—according to Moorish belief a circular place. It is formed usually of trained bay trees, grown high enough to provide shade. Within are benches and a table. The glorieta has subsequently been elaborated into a building; by the time we reach the famous example at Schönbrunn, a considerable transformation has taken place.

A belvedere is another form of building that is variously interpreted. An early eighteenth-century definition introduces another garden building term whose definition is ambiguous, 'pavilion':

at the ends and extremities of a park are beautiful pavilions of masonry, which the French call belvederes, or pavilions of Aurora, which are as pleasant to rest oneself in, after a long walk, as they are to the eye, for the handsome prospect they yield; they serve also to retire into for shelter when it rains. The word belvedere is Italian [from bel vedere], *and signifies a beauteous prospect, which is properly given to these pavilions . . . being always built upon some eminence. . . .*

A pavilion was, it seems, originally a temporary tent-like structure. There was Cleopatra's pavilion of 'cloth of gold tissue'; we were taught at school of the magnificent pavilions erected on the occasion of Henry VIII's 'Field of the Cloth of Gold', and before that, one may recall that most delightful and obviously movable structure from which the exquisite 'Dame à la Licorne' emerges in the famous sequence of French tapestries of the early sixteenth century. Its best known contemporary form is that of the cricket pavilion, which ranges from a rectangular tent to the internationally famous building at Lord's—both structures concerned with outdoor summer pleasures. By rights, surely, the eighteenth-century so-called 'Gothic tent' at Painshill in Surrey (plate 360) should be included in this genus.

Temples, in their immense variety and with their deeply religious significance, should scarcely be included as mere garden ornaments, but as buildings, copied from ancient styles, the abodes of minor deities (such as Cupid, Pope's 'genius of the place' and Vanbrugh's 'Four Winds' at Castle Howard (plate 385). These enter frequently and freely into gardens without sacrilege towards the more established deities—particularly from the eighteenth until the early twentieth century. A splendid example is James Paine's superb Temple of Diana at Weston Park, Staffordshire (plate 391), which combines an orangery leading into a tea-room and thence into a music room. (See Chapter 17.)

The grotto, now not common (many, being subterranean, having collapsed) and rarely if ever now constructed, has a distinguished and interesting part in the history of garden architecture. The historical anthropologists will no doubt associate them with primitive man's life in caves, which he decorated; they were, however, far from being mere caves—the façades in particular were considerable works of architecture, as may still be seen in a number of Italian gardens.

Like so much else that we now associate particularly with our Western world, the grotto was a feature of the Orient, though no doubt of an entirely different kind from that which we now associate with it. In the eighth century the poet Tsu Yung wrote of a grotto deep in a darksome grove. From within it he sat and contemplated the world around:

Fronting the door the South Hill looming near,
The forest mirrored in the river clear

How astonishingly this anticipates Pope's lines written just a thousand years later on his own grotto (incidentally used to house what must have been one of the earliest collections of minerals in the country):

. . . where Thames' translucent wave
Shines a broad mirrour thro' the shadowy cave

This surely indicates some deep regard that man has for the dark places within the crust of the earth, particularly when one can see reflected the consoling and inspiring gleams of light outside.

The first great era of grotto-making in Europe was during the mid sixteenth century. One of the most famous was that designed about 1552 by Primataccio for Charles, Cardinal of Lorraine. Though it disappeared long ago, it is well documented. It was cut into the side of a steep hill and reached by climbing up a path from the river. Ronsard has an eclogue on it —describing the whole world of make-believe of Gorgon's heads, Bacchus, nymphs, fauns and satyrs that surrounded it. If no cliff-side was available, as at the Tuileries in Paris, the grotto was built up from the flat.

Possibly one of the first grottoes in England was a slightly mysterious place in the basement of Inigo Jones's Banqueting House, designed by Isaac de Caux—whose relative, Saloman de Caux, was apparently concerned with the famous and highly elaborate grotto at Heidelberg Castle.

The grotto became very fashionable in the British Isles during the eighteenth and early nineteenth centuries; the famous example created by Alexander Pope (incidentally making use of an existing subterranean passage) has been mentioned. Ladies would spend many hours decorating them; again we can quote Pope on the grotto at Crux-Easton:

Here, shunning idleness at once and praise
This radiant pile nine rural sisters raise

This grotto was adorned with shell-work, that is, the laborious affixing of myriads of shells to cover the walls.

At the beginning of the last century J. C. Loudon described the grotto at Painshill as the finest in Europe. It was constructed by a certain Bushell who designed the grottoes at Wimbledon House, Oatlands, and elsewhere: he was 'the most celebrated grotto and cascade artist that ever appeared in England'. Painshill was considered his *chef d'œuvre*.

It was Loudon also, in his *Encyclopaedia*, who gave a list of the materials suitable for decorating the interiors of grottoes, which included 'shells, corals, spars, crystallizations, and other marine and mineral productions . . . to add to the effect, pieces of looking glass are inserted in different places and positions'. The grotto had indeed come down in the world since the days when creatures of classical mythology occupied Meudon, and when the statuary in the grotto at Stourhead in Wiltshire (the finest surviving British example) (plates 15 and 16) was sculptured by John Cheere.

The temples that adorned landscape gardens from the time of Stowe in Buckinghamshire in the early eighteenth century were essentially based on classical models, often taken and accurately copied from published works (again we can go to Stourhead for examples). Along with other classical monuments, they went out of fashion when, at the end of the century, Uvedale Price and Richard Payne Knight became the arbiters of garden taste:

Such buildings English nature must reject,
And claim from art th' appearance of neglect:
No decoration should we introduce,
That has not first been nat'raliz'd by use.

However, in the nineteenth century they were again permissible 'if the extent of the grounds and the expenditure on their management allow them to be of that size and of that correctness of style, which give the classic air and dignity that are their only sources of pleasure'.

The gazebo seems to be an English invention—or at least the name is. The Hon. John Byng, later Lord Torrington, who toured England at the end of the eighteenth century, considered the term was an abbreviation of 'gaze about'. Others attribute its origins to a jocular Latinization of the verb 'gaze' comparable with *videbo*. No use of the word can be found earlier than the mid eighteenth century. It is certainly applied to those buildings whence one can obtain a view—a sort of peering-point comparable with the Tudor mount—not infrequently of two storeys. Quite often they were placed not to observe the beauties of nature so much as to overlook a main road or even the village.

The age of the picturesque in the closing years of the eighteenth century and the early years of the nineteenth provided a rich variety of ornamental buildings—or utilitarian buildings disguised, usually with charming absurdity, as something else. Many books illustrating them were published by designers such as Thomas Overton, John Plaw and J. B. Papworth. Drawings of gateways, keepers' cottages, dog-kennels and ice-houses were available in every style—pointed Gothic, castellated Gothic, Greek, Roman, Egyptian and oriental. Every material was used—timber, stone, brick and cast-iron. Papworth was the most productive and certainly the most ingenious. Among the types of summer-house these and similar authors illustrated were American, Grecian, Chinese, Scottish, Italian, Polish and Russian cottages—the description of 'cottage' in these instances came under this heading of 'decorative buildings introduced more for their picturesque effect than as absolutely necessary'. John Plaw went so far as to provide in his book of aquatints the appropriate landscaped scenic background against which his buildings should be set.

One could further elaborate indefinitely and tediously on the types of garden house; what more can be said, than that they range from the sublime to the ridiculous, from the magnificent to the strictly functional, for every one of the multitude of purposes that a garden owner finds desirable.

349

349 Pavilion or tea-house in the Japanese gardens, Tully, County Kildare, Eire, laid out in 1906 by the Japanese gardener Eida.

350 Tudor garden house, octagonal in shape, at Melford Hall, Suffolk.

351 One of a pair of early seventeenth-century gazebos or garden houses at Montacute, Somerset.

352

353

354

352 A small open, temple-like gazebo on a wall at Montacute.

353 One of the twin Boycott Pavilions at Stowe, Buckinghamshire. Designed by James Gibbs about 1728, they were altered by Giovanni Battista Borra before 1763. Originally they had pyramidal roofs, but Borra replaced these with domed roofs topped by belvederes.

354 A Georgian gazebo in the corner of the walled garden at Walcot Hall, Shropshire. Hexagonal in shape, it is surmounted by a belvedere.

355 Carolean garden house with ornamental ironwork at Packwood, Warwickshire. This is one of four such buildings at the corners of the walled garden.

356 Late eighteenth-century garden house at Luton Hoo, Bedfordshire.

357 The mid eighteenth-century Banqueting House at Studley Royal, Yorkshire, restored in recent years by West Riding County Council.

358 One of the Italianate pavilions at Mereworth Castle, Kent, one of the earliest Palladian villas to be built in Britain.

359 A bathing pavilion in the Baroque style at Kelvedon Hall, Essex.

360 The wooden Gothic tent or arbour at
Painshill, Surrey. The original was
constructed in the mid eighteenth century;
this restoration dates from 1914 and is
itself now in need of restoration. It is an
octagonal structure with a vaulted ceiling.

361 Garden folly in the Gothic style, built
in the late eighteenth century at the end
of the canal at Frampton Court,
Gloucestershire.

362 The Gothic gazebo at Marston Hall,
Lincolnshire. Originally built in the
eighteenth century, it was restored in the
1960s. The Gothic façade was designed by
Mr John Partridge, ARIBA; the interior
decorations with bird motifs were done by
Miss Barbara Jones.

363 The Gothic garden house at Saltram, Devon, built in the 1760s or 1770s. It is octagonal in shape.

364 The Rustic Cottage, a feature near the lake at Stourhead, Wiltshire, has Gothic details. Its date is uncertain, but it was probably built between 1750 and 1770.

365 Duchess Georgiana's Grotto at Chatsworth, Derbyshire, built in the late eighteenth century.

366 Shell grotto, probably early nineteenth-century, at Drummond Castle, Perthshire.

367 The nineteenth-century Hermitage, at Bicton, Devon, built as a summer-house. The floor is laid with deer knuckle-bones.

368 A garden house in a tree at Pitchford Hall, Shropshire. The framework is of much earlier date than the present exterior in late eighteenth-century Gothic style.

369 Gazebo by the River Avon at Stoneleigh Abbey, Warwickshire.

370 One of a pair of twentieth-century garden houses, showing the interior, at Hidcote Bartrim Manor, Gloucestershire. They were presumably designed by Major Lawrence Johnston, an architect, who began planning this well-known garden in about 1905.

371 The Pin Mill at Bodnant, Denbighshire, was built originally at Woodchester, Gloucestershire, as a garden house. It was later used as a mill for pin manufacture and then as a tannery. In its decayed state it was bought by the 2nd Lord Aberconway, who had it moved to its present site at the end of the Canal Terrace.

372 Modern arbour, constructed in wire and twisted bars, in the gardens of The Owl House, Lamberhurst, Kent.

373

374

373 The Italian garden with its loggia at Sledmere House, Yorkshire. The house was built in 1751 but was partly destroyed by fire in 1911. An addition, made after the fire, was demolished in 1945, and this garden was constructed in its place. The statuary and busts are eighteenth-century.

374 Treillage rose arbour at the Château de Villandry, Indre-et-Loire, France.

375 Summer-house, built in 1960, at Dartington Hall, Devon. The roof is supported by Ionic columns.

376 Arbour in the garden of the Benjamin Waller House, Colonial Williamsburg, Virginia, U.S.A.

375

376

377 Arbour in the garden of the Blue Bell Tavern, Colonial Williamsburg.

378 Garden pavilion, built in 1796, at Alvöen, near Bergen, Norway.

379 Eighteenth-century well-house in the garden at Stabbestad, near Kragerö, Norway.

380 Pavilions in the small garden of the Forbidden City, Peking, China.

17 Temples

It would be in the best visual tradition to say that all temples should at first be viewed from far off, as in a Poussin painting, at the end of the long walk or cresting some hill top of the gods; that one's thoughts should be revolving around gay musical parties by a limpid stream which should always encircle a Temple of the Muses; that the senses should be enlivened by the tenuous ivy which sensuously snares the fingers as they stroke the grooved stones. Temples are essentially frivolous and mood-evoking and were often intended for no other purpose than to satisfy the great Goddess of Taste. Into them went rococo wall paintings—as at James Paine's Temple of Diana at Weston Park, Staffordshire (plate 391)—mounds of delicate tea-bowls for the Watteauesque parties, orange trees, a wise owl or two and a host of architectural frivolities.

In England the temple which was conceived with perhaps the nicest sense of proportion and position—some of those at Stourhead and Stowe apart—is the Temple of the Four Winds at Castle Howard in Yorkshire (plate 386). Designed by Sir John Vanbrugh, a competition was held to decide its interior decoration. The two Italian stuccoists Giuseppe Artari and Francesco Vassalli competed, the latter winning the day. Artari retired with two guineas for his drawings and Vassalli went on, in 1736, to enrich the interior with stucco and scagliola. Recently restored with new lead and gold-leaf, it stands at the end of a broad, statue-bedecked sward, a half-way's rest to Nicholas Hawksmoor's great Mausoleum (plate 439) a mile farther on in this grandest of parks which 'fences half the horizon'.

When in 1745 George Lyttelton turned to landscape his Hagley estate in Worcestershire, Nature had already given him considerable help, and his friend James Thomson, wandering the hill slopes as he revised part of his poem *The Seasons*, wrote of 'the most agreeable place and company in the world'. Soon there was to be a ruined castle to earn for itself praise in being regarded as part of a truly medieval past—but it was 1758 before Lyttelton asked James 'Athenian' Stuart, who had recently made a tour of Greece with his friend Nicholas Revett, to design a Temple of Theseus.

The mood of the time was for innovation and change. Robert Adam was back from Italy ready to fling the mantle of neo-classicism over all before him. At Stowe in Buckinghamshire the Queen's Temple, an early and dull work, probably by James Gibbs, and built in 1744, was changed thirty years later into one of proportion and grace by the addition of a portico on four graceful Corinthian columns. The interior is later still. At Stourhead in Wiltshire, when Dr Pococke visited it in 1754 two pieces of water were soon 'to be made into one and much enlarged'; there was the Temple of Flora (plate 383) to visit, beside the Paradise Well with its busts after the antique representing Flora and her attendants. Of the Pantheon here (plate 382) even the critical Horace Walpole was moved to record that 'few buildings exceed the magnificence, taste and beauty of the temple'. The works it enshrined were by Michael Rysbrack and John Cheere, or were brought from Herculaneum. Worship might be made also in pagan fashion to the sun and the moon; the lovely circular Temple of the Sun at Stourhead (plate 384) is copied from that at Baalbec in Syria, and the mason Robert Doe when creating the Temple of the Moon, or of Piety (1728), at Studley Royal, Yorkshire (plate 381), studied seventeenth-century engravings of classical temples.

The Temple of the Sun can only be approached by a grotto-like bridge. On its heights, surrounded by dense trees and looking out over the lake, we realize why Walpole wrote of 'the most picturesque scenes in the world'. Full circle to our day-dreams. The punt has bumped the lichened stone of temple rising sheer from mirrored water. The mind grasps at the ideal garden of dreams. It should be composed of lawns and walks and slopes, of the clear reflections of lakes, of woods, plantations, wildernesses and glades. There should be rocks, bridges, grottoes and cascades. But most of all there should be many temples fairly placed, dedicated to Bacchus or Diana or the gilded Sun and full of the images of devils and gods of the heathen, with wreathing votive smoke and frescoed ceilings. Wherever in the world one finds them, temples should be just this, or more.

381 The Temple of Piety, Studley Royal, Yorkshire.

382 The Pantheon at Stourhead, Wiltshire, a small-scale adaptation of the original in Rome, but differing in certain major details.

383 The Temple of Flora, with its Doric portico, at Stourhead. In front is the urn above the head of Paradise Well. This temple and those illustrated in plates 382 and 384 were designed for Henry Hoare by Henry Flitcroft and erected in the mid eighteenth century.

384

385

386

384 The Temple of the Sun (or of Apollo), at Stourhead, derived from the original at Baalbec in Syria.

385 The octagonal Gothic Temple built in 1750 at Bramham Park, Yorkshire.

386 Sir John Vanbrugh's Temple of the Four Winds, designed between 1724 and 1726 for the 3rd Earl of Carlisle, at Castle Howard, Yorkshire. The building has four Ionic porticoes and a richly decorated interior. On the right is a distant view of Hawksmoor's Mausoleum.

387 The Ionic temple at the north-west end of the Rievaulx Terrace, Duncombe Park, Yorkshire, possibly designed by Sir Thomas Robinson and erected in 1758. The coved ceiling is richly decorated with paintings of mythological scenes by Giovanni Borgnis (Burnici).

387

388 At the southern end of the half-mile-long Rievaulx Terrace is this Doric temple, again possibly designed by Sir Thomas Robinson and dating from the same period.

389 The temple in the Gothic Revival style at Stowe, Buckinghamshire. Designed by James Gibbs, it was built in the 1740s. There are still nine temples in the grounds at Stowe, but the remainder are classical in conception.

390 The temple at Nuneham Park, Oxfordshire, designed by the 1st Earl Harcourt, with some assistance from James ('Athenian') Stuart, in the 1760s. Despite its classical appearance it houses the parish church, replacing a medieval church on the same site.

391 The Temple of Diana, designed by James Paine, *c.* 1770, in Weston Park, Staffordshire.

390

391

392 The temple in the Italian Garden at
Bicton, Devon. The Italian Garden was
laid out in 1735, allegedly to a design by
André le Nôtre (who died in 1700);
presumably the temple dates from this
period.

393 Tuscan temple in the garden of
Hinton Ampner House, Hampshire.

394 to 398 Five variations on a theme:

   394 A Temple of Love in the Italian
garden at Compton Acres, Dorset.

395 Mique's Temple d'Amour at Le Petit Trianon, Versailles, France, built for Marie Antoinette soon after the accession of her husband, Louis XVI. The somewhat flattened dome is supported by ten Corinthian columns.

396 A type designed in the late nineteenth century with a wrought-iron cupola and a statue of Cupid in the centre. Similar structures with a statue of Atlanta were designed by Harold Peto and became known as Temples of Atlanta.

397 A similar temple in the Fountain
Garden, Longwood, Pennsylvania,
U.S.A.

398 A modern version at the Villa
Taranto, Pallanza, Italy.

399 The Temple of Mon Plaisir,
Christinegaard, Bergen, Norway, built
c. 1820.

400 Early nineteenth-century Temple of
Flora in the garden at Hövik, near Oslo,
Norway. It is a wooden structure covered
with birch bark.

18 Orangeries

Orangeries were the predecessors of the conservatory in Britain in the seventeenth and eighteenth centuries. They were, as is obvious, first constructed for the growing of the orange and lemon trees which are said to have been introduced in the sixteenth century. Many of them were well-proportioned buildings in stone. The heating problem was not satisfactorily solved until the nineteenth century. The first experiments were carried out by constructing a complicated system of brick flues, ranging for a distance of fifty feet within brick cavity walls. A method used in the orangery of the Apothecaries Garden at Chelsea in 1684 was a form of under-floor heating with red-hot coals shovelled beneath gratings set into the floor. Glass roofs were first installed in these orangeries in 1717, and experiments in their pitch and design were carried out towards the middle and end of the eighteenth century by the gardeners Abercrombie and Speechly in England, and by Kyle and Nicol in Scotland. Hot-water systems were first used in France, and were brought over by the French *émigré* Count Chabannes in 1816 and used at Sundridge Park in Kent.

It was, however, the enterprise and skill of William Atkinson of Paddington, who finally improved and cheapened the processes, which made possible the astonishing development of glass-houses and domestic conservatories in Victorian England; these ranged from the huge 300-foot structure of Paxton's Crystal Palace to the elegant heated fern cases used in Victorian drawing-rooms.

Orangeries are to be found—now largely decayed or adapted for other purposes—in the grounds of the great English and Scottish estates. They were designed by such architects as Sir Christopher Wren, whose orangery at Kensington Palace can still be seen and enjoyed, and by Sir William Chambers, whose structure at Kew Gardens is now a museum. What is now a tea-house at Ham House was once an orangery visited and praised by John Evelyn. Wren's beautiful example at Hampton Court was first a banqueting-house and was converted to its new use in 1760. Possibly one of the largest and most elaborate buildings of this kind is the French-style orangery at Wrest Park, Bedfordshire, which was built in 1836 and sited on a high grass bank.

Other examples which still survive in Britain are Stockman's elegant structure at Saltram House, Devon (plate 404), and orangeries at Dyrham, Gloucestershire (plate 407), the semicircular Doric example at Osterley

Park, Middlesex (plate 408), and good examples at Belton House, Lincolnshire (plate 406), and Powis Castle, Montgomeryshire (plate 401). A baroque example worth mentioning is the 'orangerie' in the Château Weikersheim, near Bad Mergentheim.

Though these types of garden buildings are out of fashion, Sir Edwin Lutyens reproduced a classical example of an old orangery at Hestercombe in Somerset, in 1904; largely, one suspects, as a decorative garden ornament.

The buildings which shelter them may no longer be built, but orange trees in cases or boxes are still planted and used for decoration. Visitors to Versailles are familiar with the regular rows of these trees assembled in the lower court by the Hundred Steps. Provided such trees are protected in winter and their foliage well sprayed, though less hardy than bay they form an admirable feature in a paved courtyard.

Finally, perhaps, it might be said that the most modern example of such structures is the 175-foot dome, designed by Richard Buckminster Fuller, in the Botanical Garden of St Louis, Missouri. This is the 'Climatron', built of aluminium tubing and an acrylic plastic skin with devices for controlling the environment for both tropical and alpine plants.

401 The late eighteenth-century orangery at Powis Castle, Montgomeryshire, restored in recent years by the National Trust and once more used to house plants.

402 The orangery at Dumbarton Oaks, Washington D.C., U.S.A.

403 Dating from about 1700, the orangery at Montacute, Somerset, has been restored by the National Trust. The obelisk finials are repeated elsewhere in the garden.

404 Built between 1773 and 1774, and once thought to be by Robert Adam, the orangery at Saltram, Devon, another restoration by the National Trust, was designed by Stockman. It is one of the few in which orange and lemon trees are actually grown. In their tubs they are moved out of doors for the summer.

403

404

255

405

406

405 The eighteenth-century orangery (called the 'Palm House') at Ripley Castle, Yorkshire.

406 Designed by Sir Jeffry Wyatville, the great orangery at Belton House, Lincolnshire, now referred to as the Camellia House and used as a tea-room for visitors, was built between 1819 and 1820.

407 The orangery at Dyrham Park, Gloucestershire, built about 1702. The slate roof was replaced by glass a century or so later. This, too, has been restored by the National Trust and is used as a tea-room. It is called 'The Greenhouse'.

408 Robert Adam's orangery built in the latter part of the eighteenth century in Osterley Park, Middlesex.

19 Chinoiserie and Japonaiserie

In 1749 Mrs Elizabeth Montagu wrote that 'sick of Grecian elegance and symmetry, or Gothic grandeur and magnificence, we must all seek the barbarous gaudy goüt of the Chinese: and fat-headed Pagods, and shaking Mandarins, bear the prize from the finest works of antiquity'. In 1762 Lord Kames similarly claimed, not without displeasure, that the Chinese manner was preferred before that of Greece and the Gothic.

By that time W. and J. Halfpenny's *Rural Architecture in the Chinese Taste* and Sir William Chambers's more significant *Designs of Chinese Buildings* of 1757 had been produced. In 1772 Chambers's much more unsubstantiated *Dissertation on Oriental Gardening* was issued.

All this resulted in a vogue for garden ornament in a style far remote from the genuine thing—the entertaining mannerism called chinoiserie.

Rather surprisingly, the Chinese fashion was linked in the French mind with the free style of the English landscape garden. Between 1776 and 1784 G. L. Le Rouge published his volumes of designs *Jardins Anglo-Chinois*, apparently unaware that, for example, the Rev. William Mason, Capability Brown's poetical publicist, was extremely critical of the Chinese style. By 1794 the critic of taste Richard Payne Knight so despised the Chinese manner that his artist Thomas Hearne included a Chinese bridge in a scene to illustrate the defects of a bad landscape design. Chinoiserie, therefore, did not have a long fashion in British gardening. Nor are its remains frequently encountered: much of it—for example the wooden bridges—was inevitably of a transient nature. There are today better examples of it on the Continent.

In 1756, however, a writer named James Cawthorn wrote with satirical exaggeration:

On every hill a spire-crowned temple swells
Hung round with serpents and a fringe of bells . . .

As the pagoda in various forms—mostly far remote from its origins—remains an oriental feature that is still found as a garden ornament, it might be well to summarize its history. Strictly speaking it is a Hindu or Chinese sacred tower, the name coming to us from the Portuguese *pagode*. It was originally a purely religious Indian building, but was adapted by the Chinese not only as a mausoleum for relics of Buddha but also as an ornamental building, usually situated among rock-work. According to Josiah Conder (*Landscape Gardening in Japan*), these pagodas—narrow stone buildings of up to five or even more storeys—spread to Japan where they became purely decorative features in the landscape gardens, presenting a very picturesque appearance set amid the foliage, imparting the suggestion of actual landscape on a diminutive scale.

He illustrates examples in ancient gardens, adding that the Japanese call them Korean towers, the arts of China having first reached that country by way of Korea. The designer, he informs us, was allowed much more freedom than when working on other buildings. Not infrequently European buildings of this type in the Chinese manner were, and still are, called kiosks—a word of Turkish origin attached to open-air buildings. Nowadays this word is much more closely related to our modern conception of, for example, an ice-cream vendor's stall; but once it was assumed to have an oriental and exotic meaning. In the same way, the Victorians debased the meaning of pagoda to that place where Rhoda sold 'ice-creams, whisky and soda'.

But before that time a number of chinoiserie pagodas had been built, some of which remain. The very substantial structure by Sir William Chambers at Kew Gardens (plate 409), of about 1761, is world famous. There are the Chinese buildings at Sans Souci, Potsdam, and at Schloss Nymphenburg, Munich, both in Germany (plate 418). There is the Kiosque de l'Impératrice set among roses at the Château Bagatelle in Paris (plate 417). But these are only minor features compared with the wealth of classical and even Gothic garden buildings which are so liberally scattered over the gardens of the landscape and the picturesque eras. One of the last chinoiserie pagodas to be erected—still standing, though never completed in the form that was originally intended—is the stone and cast-iron building in the fantastic garden laid out by the Earl of Shrewsbury in the opening years of the last century at Alton Towers in North Staffordshire (plate 410). It is short of three tiers originally planned and the forty ornate Chinese gas lamps (fed from a gas-holder within the building) that were first intended.

Surprisingly, japonaiserie was of a much later introduction—not until the 1860s when Japan was opened to the West and such plant collectors as John Gould Veitch and Robert Fortune brought back so many of the typical Japanese florist's flowers. Unlike chinoiserie, japonaiserie was not a diversion lightly undertaken but a matter of serious art that by 1885 had earned the satire of Gilbert's *Mikado*. Japanese garden designers came to Europe to work in their own traditions, or earnest-souled persons read the works of Josiah Conder, Lafcadio Hearn and others who had lived in Japan and studied its garden art with great seriousness. Little remains of their work, however—an occasional temple (perhaps the genuine article imported), a lantern or two, and now and then a stork may be found. But the lessons of the Japanese garden are today to be found more in its spirit than in its ornaments, although an occasional modern example is constructed under Japanese supervision.

409 The octagonal Chinese pagoda at the Royal Botanic Gardens, Kew, Surrey, designed by Sir William Chambers and erected between 1761 and 1762. It is 163 feet high.

410 The Pagoda Fountain at Alton Towers, Staffordshire, built in the first half of the nineteenth century. The original design was intended to be even more elaborate. The fountain jet soars seventy feet into the air above the pagoda.

411 Japanese 'Snow Scene' lantern in the Japanese Garden at Compton Acres, Dorset, designed by a Japanese architect in the 1920s.

412 and 413 Two of the figures in the Japanese Garden at Compton Acres, Dorset.

414 Part of the Japanese Garden at Tatton Park, Cheshire, laid out about 1910.

415 Japanese lantern of the Kasuga type in the Japanese Gardens, Tully, County Kildare, Eire, laid out by the Japanese gardener Eida in 1906.

416 The Chinese bridge at Wrest Park, Bedfordshire. This once formed part of a 'willow pattern' scene, laid out in the late 1830s, but the temple has long since disappeared.

417 The Kiosque de l'Impératrice at the
Château Bagatelle, Paris, France,
showing oriental influence.

418 The Pagodenburg in the grounds of
Schloss Nymphenburg, Munich, West
Germany.

419 A kiosk or garden house showing
oriental influence, at Schloss
Nymphenburg.

420 Ornamental rock in the small garden of the Forbidden City, Peking, China.

421 Pavilion in Peihai Park, Peking.

422 Bronze birds and beasts in the gardens of the Summer Palace, Peking.

266

423 In the garden of Daisen-In, Daitokuji Temple, Kyoto, Japan; an example of the 'dry landscape' style.

20 Aviaries, Dovecotes and Columbaria

'As for Aviaries, I like them not, except they are of that Largeness, as they be turfed and having Living Plants and Bushes set in them; that the Birds may have more scope and Naturall Neastling and that no Foulness appears in the Floor of the Aviary'—a sentiment or an opinion of Lord Bacon's with which most of us would be in agreement no doubt. Many of the aviaries built in the grounds of the great seventeenth- and eighteenth-century estates have now disappeared, but nineteenth-century English examples still survive, notably the Chinese aviary at Dropmore House, Buckinghamshire, and the pheasant aviary at Waddesdon Manor in the same county. Neither of them adheres to Lord Bacon's specification, but they were designed as decorative features in the landscape rather than to provide an ideal environment for their inhabitants.

On the other hand the great aviaries in the zoological gardens of most modern capitals would have pleased his lordship. Flight cages of a very large size were constructed in the 1920s, notably in San Diego, California, where the largest of all birds, the Andean condor, has been bred in captivity. The most recent and perhaps the most notable of these great aviaries is at Regent's Park Zoo, designed by Lord Snowdon and the architect Cedric Price, and using a system of construction pioneered by Buckminster Fuller, through which the public may walk on an overhead ramp.

Methods of enclosure have been evolved in the U.S.A. using a principle that birds will naturally congregate in a lighted area rather than in darkness. In St Louis Zoological Gardens an illuminated garden has been designed complete with tropical plants, pool and stream into which the public can look and enjoy the sight of the birds from a darkened hall with only a low barrier separating the two sections. The zoo at Antwerp, Belgium, has tried a similar illusion by constructing cages of a thin and nearly invisible steel mesh.

In medieval times no feudal lord's establishment was complete without its columbaria or pigeon houses. These buildings were either circular or square with gabled roofs. The interior was designed with tiers of nesting-boxes which might house any number from 500 to 1,000 birds. A fine example is the circular dovecote at Rousham, Oxfordshire. Other English examples can be seen in the southern counties, particularly in Sussex, Somerset and Cornwall. The fifteenth-century buttressed dovecote at Athelhampton, Dorset (plate 424), is particularly notable.

Some of the oldest surviving examples are to be found in Scotland, in the counties of Midlothian and West Lothian.

No fewer than twenty-one are listed as monuments. They are certainly worth preserving for their historical interest as well as for their unique appearance.

The barrel dovecotes on high posts, which are so popular today, are erected not as a source of game but to house the many varieties of ornamental breeds of pigeon which are now available, such as pouters, tumblers, fantails, frillbacks and jacobins. Aviaries with outdoor covered flight cages are also to be found now in gardens, housing varieties of finch, lovebirds, ornamental pheasants and budgerigars, as well as Australian parrots and cockatoos. Aviculture is in fact an inexpensive hobby which attracts many amateurs and is as popular today as it was in Roman times.

424 The fifteenth-century dovecote at Athelhampton, Dorset, which has about a thousand nesting holes.

425 The Saxon dove-house at Charleston Manor, Sussex, reputed to be over a thousand years old.

426 The ancient dovecote or columbarium at Cotehele, Cornwall, restored in 1962 by the National Trust.

427 Part of the great aviary at Dropmore, Buckinghamshire, thought to have been built in the early 1850s. Built in the Chinese style, the base, pilasters and cornice are made of pierced green faience tiles, the main supports are of ironwork painted red.

428 Dovecote at Hotvedt, Drammen, Norway, built in the latter half of the nineteenth century.

429 Dovecote and well-head in the grounds of the restored Tryon Palace, New Bern, North Carolina. The dovecote has been rebuilt in the style of that originally designed by John Hawkes of London for the Royal Governor, Josiah Martin.

21 Bridges

'The bridge,' wrote J. C. Loudon in his *Encyclopaedia of Gardening* (1822), 'is one of the grandest decorations of garden-scenery.' And it is true that although bridges were at first necessary for providing crossings at streams and moats, they later, particularly in the seventeenth and eighteenth centuries, became important decorative features. Sometimes watercourses were diverted or specially made to provide excuse for their erection.

Early bridges survive in some medieval towns. Bruges (the very name means 'bridges') has many of great charm, such as the Pont Saint-Boniface, leading from an avenue of clipped limes in the grounds of the Church of Our Lady to the grounds of the Gruuthuse through a delightful little arched outhouse. Here water, trees, stone, brick and cobbles combine to afford us a rare glimpse of medieval garden architecture in an authentic setting.

Some drawbridges, once a defensive necessity, still survive as decorative elements in English castle gardens. Hever Castle (noted for its Italian gardens) has one over its moat, near a display of topiary. A Jacobean moat bridge is at Blickling Hall in Norfolk (Robert Lyminge, *c.* 1616–27), with balustrades pierced with designs reminiscent of strap-work. A stone moat bridge of four arches stands at the earlier (sixteenth-century) part of Hampton Court Palace, though the moat itself has been carpeted with lawns since the time of Charles II. From the bridge's castellated walls rise eight columns, on each of which sits one of the Queen's beasts (modern); 159 such beasts, carved in wood, stood in the gardens here in the sixteenth century.

Of classical bridges, one of the finest of all is at Chatsworth (1762), built by order of the 4th Duke of Devonshire as part of the plan to landscape the older formal garden. It is a dignified structure of three large arches, with a classical balustrade and with statues on its piers. A simpler bridge (1749) at Stourhead forms part of the landscape scheme of which the lake is the centre, and across which may be seen the Pantheon, built *c.* 1753 (plate 382). The *mise en scène* was celebrated in verse:

Throughout the various scenes above, below,
Lawns, walks, and slopes, with verdant carpets glow:
On the clear mirror float the inverted shades
Of woods, plantations, wildernesses, glades,
Rocks, bridges, temples, grottos and cascades.

But the finest and most delightful of all classical bridges are those of the eighteenth-century Palladian type—bridges, that is, with superstructures after designs by Palladio—the prototype of which is at Wilton, Wiltshire (1737), designed by the 9th Earl of Pembroke and Roger Morris (plate 431). It is conceived as a covered temple, the centre of which has a straight entablature supported by Ionic columns. At each end is a pavilion with arches, columns and pediments. Variations on the same design are at Stowe (before 1744) (plate 432) and Prior Park, Bath (1750; probably by Capability Brown). There is another at Blenheim (plate 430), designed by Vanbrugh, but its superstructure was never added. A fourth, constructed at Hagley, Worcestershire (1764), no longer exists. A simpler wooden version is at Scampston Park in Yorkshire (c. 1773; attributed to Brown or Holland).

Also worth noting is D. Garrett's bridge at Castle Howard, which spans the New River, and was built in the 1740s for the 3rd Earl of Carlisle (plate 439).

Bridges are an essential feature of Japanese gardens. To the Japanese, his garden is a quasi-religious scheme, its every detail expressing a way of life. The garden itself may represent mountains, valleys or woodlands, or perhaps seascapes and islands, in which case it may consist of rocks and sand only. The bridge is a significant symbol and may represent a mystical union by joining two parts of the garden. A fine wooden bridge, almost semicircular, is in the garden of Kameido Shrine, Tokyo, but there is one in almost every Japanese garden. Japanese bridges are sometimes used in European gardens, as, for example, at Powerscourt, Co. Kildare, Ireland. And the painter Monet had one in his garden at Giverny.

Bridges are almost as essential in Dutch gardens, but there they have no mystical significance and merely provide crossings over waterways.

But of all places, few equal Cambridge for its garden bridges. As the Cam flows through college grounds it is spanned in each by a bridge; it may be the wooden bridge of Queens'; the stone bridge of Clare, the oldest of them all (1638–40); the Gothic cast-iron footbridge over a little tributary between Trinity and St John's; or the romantic St John's 'Bridge of Sighs' (Henry Hutchinson, 1831). Whether one drifts beneath them in a punt or walks over them, they add enchantment to the formal views on either side.

430 Sir John Vanbrugh's Grand Bridge
at Blenheim Palace, Oxfordshire, begun
in 1710. The lake was formed in the late
1750s by Lancelot Brown from the little
River Glyme.

431 The Palladian bridge at Wilton House, Wiltshire, designed by the 9th Earl of Pembroke and erected by Roger Morris. Building was completed in 1737.

432 The Palladian bridge at Stowe, Buckinghamshire, completed before 1744. Although it is closely copied from that at Wilton it differs in that it was designed for carriage traffic instead of pedestrians and therefore lacks the stepped approaches. The keystones of the arches are carved with masks, whereas those of the Wilton bridge are plain.

433 The five-arched Palladian bridge at
Stourhead, Wiltshire, built in 1763 and
based on Palladio's bridge at Vicenza.

277

434

435

436

434 The 'Roman' bridge at Weston Park, Staffordshire, designed by James Paine, *c.* 1770.

435 The 'Chippendale' bridge at Pusey House, Berkshire.

436 A simple wooden bridge over the moat at Barrington Court, Somerset.

437 Simple bridge in the grounds of the Katsura Detached Palace, Kyoto, Japan.

438 Mid nineteenth-century bridge at Eastwell Park, Kent. The arcaded balustrading is repeated on the park walls and elsewhere.

22 The Darker Side

Our blessed Saviour chose the garden sometimes for his oratory, and dying, for the place of his sepulchre; and we do vouch for many weighty causes, that there are none more fit to bury our dead in, than in our gardens . . . where our beds may be decked and carpeted with verdant and fragrant flowers, trees and perennial plants, the most natural and instructive hieroglyphics of our expected resurrection and immortality . . .

Thus wrote the diarist John Evelyn, adding that he would like his own body so to be buried: he had already mentioned that the heart of the statesman and man of letters, Sir William Temple, had been interred in his garden. There is today a burial ground in the gardens of Mount Stewart in Northern Ireland (plate 443). One could produce a number of other instances of those who were buried in gardens, particularly during the landscape period. Jean-Jacques Rousseau's body was first buried on the Island of Poplars in the garden at Ermenonville, the garden of his patron, Girardin; and G. F. Meyer, the landscape artist who had helped Girardin, was buried on an adjoining island. Ernst Ludwig, Duke of Gotha, who died in 1804, was also buried in his garden, without ceremony, with no other memorial than the tree that his son was instructed to plant over his body.

As a contrast to this anonymity, one of the finest buildings adorning a landscape in the British Isles is the mausoleum of the Howard family at Castle Howard in Yorkshire (plate 439). Begun in 1731, it stands also as a memorial to Nicholas Hawksmoor—perhaps his finest work—who did not live to see its completion. In conjunction with Vanbrugh's Temple of the Four Winds (plate 386), and the bridge of a rather later date over the New River, it forms a group of essentially 'garden' buildings on the grandest scale, once described by Sacheverell Sitwell as, of their kind, 'as beautiful as anything in Europe'.

This group of buildings aspires; on the really dark side was the garden made by the genial and prosperous Jonathan Tyers, owner of the Vauxhall pleasure gardens at Denbies, near Dorking in Surrey. Francis Hayman was apparently the designer. Following a prescribed route, one saw the episodes in the life of man, with, it seems, particular emphasis on its awful conclusion. At the end an iron gate led into the Valley of the Shadow of Death; the columns of the portico were skull-surmounted coffins.

Most frequent of once lively creatures now embedded in the cold soil of gardens are the bodies of dogs—with rather fewer horses. At Newstead Abbey in Northamptonshire is the urn-topped memorial to Lord Byron's dog, Boatswain—with a famous inscription comparing mankind to the dog, much in the latter's favour. Byron himself wished his body to join that of his dog. At Rousham in Oxfordshire, playing an important part in the masterly design of this early landscape, is the memorial to Ringwood, an otter hound of 'extraordinary sagacity' (plate 444). Of more recent history, many of the multitude of visitors to Longleat in Wiltshire must know the considerable dogs' cemetery there.

In a sense, a number of the monuments in early landscape could be classified under this heading, being memorials rather than follies. There is, for example, at Stowe, Kent's Temple of British Worthies.

The crumbling inscription of many a garden obelisk, too, recalls the dead: for some reason a favourite subject was the sad death of George IV's daughter Charlotte, who married Leopold of Saxe-Coburg and died in childbirth. The obelisk in the garden of Chiswick House in Middlesex is rather different, for the base includes a Roman tombstone of the second century showing a husband, wife and child.

The sarcophagus is rather a collector's piece than a true garden ornament, yet how admirably it does fit into that category can be seen at Iford Manor in Wiltshire, where there are three, two Roman and one Greek (plate 442).

Memorial gardens, or rather the ornamentation of them, should be mentioned. A particularly good example is the pergola-like memorial walk recently completed in the quiet churchyard of Overbury, near Tewkesbury, in Gloucestershire.

Finally, we are left with the problem of urns. Many urns are, or were, vases for the reception of the ashes of the dead. But for the correct determination and identification of these we must refer the reader to antiquarian authorities on funerary furniture.

439

440

439 Hawksmoor's Mausoleum, built between 1731 and 1742 for the 3rd Earl of Carlisle at Castle Howard, Yorkshire.

440 Memorial to William, Duke of Hamilton, in Hamilton High Parks, Lanarkshire.

441 Sarcophagus and plaque at Hever Castle, Kent, dating from the middle of the second century A.D. The relief depicts the Labours of Hercules. The plaque is possibly the end of a sarcophagus. On the right is a male figure, possibly Adonis; on the left a female figure (? Venus); in the centre a boar emerging from a cave. Both were formerly at the Villa Borghese, Rome.

442 Greek sarcophagus in the garden of Iford Manor, Wiltshire, dating from the third century B.C.

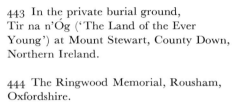

443 In the private burial ground,
Tir na n'Óg ('The Land of the Ever
Young') at Mount Stewart, County Down,
Northern Ireland.

444 The Ringwood Memorial, Rousham,
Oxfordshire.

445 Heads of mythical beasts at
Wallington, Northumberland.

446 Part of 'Valhalla' in the Abbey Gardens, Tresco, Isles of Scilly, the last resting place of numerous ship's figureheads, name-boards and other relics of ships wrecked on and around the islands. They have been restored in recent years by a team of experts under Mr H. R. Allen.

23 The Lighter Side

The step from the sublime to the ridiculous is but a short one, and the gardener who sets out to ornament his garden without due thought does so at his own peril, for to slip on that step is all too easy. It is particularly easy if the garden is a small one, for any form of ornament must then be chosen with the greatest care.

Yet there are those among us who consciously, perhaps even a little self-consciously, set out to turn a small garden into something quite out of the ordinary by the use of objects of various kinds. And, where the matter has been considered deeply and the touch is sure, the result can be most successful. What might have been an ordinary garden, or a somewhat dull corner of a garden, can be thus transformed.

If one has money, wit, discrimination and space in which to indulge one's whims, then, of course, one might produce another Bomarzo (plate 458) —if that were possible—or vie with Portmeirion, Sir Clough Williams-Ellis's pretty garden village in Merionethshire, one of the finest of twentieth-century conceits, illustrated in various photographs in this book. But a great deal of money, though pleasant to have, no doubt, is not really necessary, nor is a great deal of space needed. For example, the late Edwin Smith, some of whose sensitive photographs illuminate this book, made an enchanting little 'folly' in his small, narrow back garden in Saffron Walden with simple materials such as white-painted wood, pieces of carved stone from a ruined church and painted metal furniture. And it would not be difficult to find a hundred small gardens in London and other cities in which what another contributor has called 'engaging trifles' have been used effectively.

Looking at some of the photographs from which those in this book have been chosen, one is tempted to think that in many a gardener there is a humourist struggling to get out. There is no reason why we should take our gardening over-seriously, for gardens are for people, not the other way round. Yet humour in gardening can be a dangerous thing; a subtle alteration in the positioning of an object can, for instance, change what might have been considered a pleasantly amusing scene into something quite different, quite banal.

The desire which many gardeners have to ornament their gardens with small colourful objects might, perhaps, be compared with the way in which gypsies decorate their caravans or in which bargees used to decorate their canal boats. But, alas, it is seldom as successful; the true feeling of folk art is lacking, mass-produced gnomes, rabbits and similar objects abound, and the utilitarian but decorative staddle stones are now produced in concrete, painted white, and stand, more often than not, on coloured concrete slabs. Time and the elements will, one fears, have little effect on these, scarcely blurring their lineaments as they have blurred, often to advantage, those of many an older garden statue.

The humorous possibilities of fountains appealed to a more robust age but are not, it seems, exploited nowadays. It is just as well, perhaps, for few of us retain into later life the appreciation of practical jokes. However, it is still possible to find examples of topiary which are something less than serious in intention and execution. There is, for instance, a cottage in yew, complete with chimney stack and pot, in a garden by the roadside near Newent, Gloucestershire, and at Beckington, Somerset, there is a model of H.M.S. *Queen Elizabeth* in topiary (plate 450). These are scarcely 'humorous', as are some of the topiary birds and beasts one sees occasionally, such as those in box at Chastleton House, Oxfordshire, or the hounds forever chasing the fox along the top of the hedge at Knightshayes Court in Devon (plate 311), which bring to mind, perhaps, lines from Keats's 'Ode on a Grecian Urn'. But they serve to show that some gardeners, at least, are not bound by convention and that there are other things which can be produced in vegetable sculpture besides peacocks.

Some of the illustrations in this chapter are offered without comment; the reader is left to supply his own caption.

447 One of the collection of plaster models of prehistoric monsters arranged around the lower lake at the Crystal Palace, Sydenham, London, by Sir Joseph Paxton in the early 1850s.

448

449

450

451

450 The 'Beckington battleship'. Cut in yew in the early 1960s, it forms a hedge in a garden in Beckington, Somerset. It is based on H.M.S. *Queen Elizabeth* in which the topiarist served in the last war.

452 Last use for an old barrow.

452

453

454

455

456 The fountain at Schloss Herren-
chiemsee, near Frankfurt, ringed with
newts, tortoises and lizards.

456

457 In a public garden at Medrano, Italy.

458 Some of the so-called monsters of
Bomarzo, north-east of Viterbo, Italy,
rediscovered in recent years. The figures,
cut from the living rock, form part of a
sacred wood, the idea and execution of
which were the responsibility of
Pierfrancesco Orsini in the mid sixteenth
century.

459 Lion water jet, about six inches high,
in the garden of the Caliph's Palace,
Damascus.

460 In a small courtyard garden in
Holland.

Index